The Essence of Floral Creativity

A LEGACY

The Essence of
Floral Creativity

A LEGACY

From the works of
Bob Thomas

EDITED BY
JUNE WOOD
AND
MARGE PURNELL

Published by
THE NATIONAL COUNCIL OF STATE GARDEN CLUBS, INC.
4401 Magnolia Avenue • St. Louis, Missouri 63110-3492

Printed in the United States of America by
Columbus Productions, Inc.
Columbus, Georgia

First printing 1999

ISBN 0-941994-12-0

TABLE OF CONTENTS

This book is a tribute by
National Council of State Garden Clubs, Inc.
to Robert Clay Thomas

BOB THOMAS
July 15, 1930 - September 28, 1997

Robert Clay Thomas devoted his entire career to bringing beauty to life through his magical use of the living medium, plant material. A native of Kentucky, later a resident of Tennessee, and finally of Florida, he shared his artistic talents throughout the hemisphere through programs, schools, symposiums and his own American Guild of Flower Arrangers, which he founded and headed from 1974 to 1997.

All of his life Bob continued to study and to teach both Oriental and American styles of flower arranging, sharing his expertise as a National Council of State Garden Clubs, Inc. Instructor of Design, Ohara School Master Third Degree, and Teacher of the Ikenobo School.

His organizational and administrative skills benefited not only the NCSGC Flower Show Schools Committee and its programs, but also all levels of garden club work in the states and Regions where he lived and taught. He was a vital member of the 1997 *Handbook for Flower Shows* Revision Committee, and the originator of many new design styles that were introduced in the 1987 and 1997 editions of the *Handbook*.

Considered a pioneer in abstract floral design, he brought his discriminating sense of color and dramatic flair for creativity to this new and complex field. His gentle touch as he manipulated each leaf and blossom into a living sculpture showed deep reverence for his medium. The result was a lifetime of invitations to return again and again wherever he had been a guest speaker.

The

National Council of State Garden Clubs, Inc.

The Officers of National Council of State Garden Clubs, Inc.
on this 21st Day of September, 1997
hereby confer upon our esteemed colleague,

ROBERT C. THOMAS

the one and only Epitome of Excellence Award.
This action, taken for the first time in the history
of this organization is warranted because he is:

R ecipient of our respect and devotion
O riginator of new ideas
B enevolent donor of material for a book
E ver dependable servant of NCSGC
R educer of red tape
T ower of strength we draw upon

C ourageous speaker on controversial issues

T horoughly dedicated to integrity
H ero with a heart of gold
O ngoing devotee of openness
M entor for multitudes
A dvocate of artistic concepts
S ensibility personified

President, NCSGC, Inc.

FOREWORD

Bob Thomas was loved for his winning personality and his infectious laughter. He had a wonderful eye for proportion, balance and scale, and he possessed an extraordinary sense of color. He transformed plant material into works of art.

Probably he was most loved and will be best remembered as a teacher. Bob enlightened and inspired us. He influenced and enriched our lives.

As a tribute to him, National Council of State Garden Clubs, Inc. is proud to present this book, a written record of his teachings and a visual remembrance of his artistic talent.

His legacy lives on.

Barbara Barnette
President
National Council of State Garden Clubs, Inc.

PREFACE

Two weeks prior to his death, Bob Thomas, beloved designer and teacher, assembled the materials used in this book, and presented them to National Council of State Garden Clubs as a gift. His expressed desire was that all of his writings and photographs of his designs be compiled into a book, and that ownership of the book, with permission to reprint, be given to National Council of State Garden Clubs, Inc.

Carrying out his wishes, the book was edited by those whom he designated, June Wood and Marge Purnell. The text and pictures will attest to his unique artistry and his reverence for plant materials.

Since materials contained in this book cover several decades of Bob's design work, *Handbook for Flower Shows* requirements may have changed in the interim. In instances where this may occur, the current edition of the *Handbook* in its entirety takes precedence.

ACKNOWLEDGMENTS

June Wood
Editor

Marge Purnell
Editor

Addie Lou Harris
Coordinator

Deen Day Smith
Coordinator

Jo and Edgar Williams
Advisors

Bonnie and Stewart Allan
Photography

Joyce Droege
Photography

CHAPTER ONE

Evolution of the American Way with Flowers

When one views a flower show today, it is hard to believe that in the early decades of the 20th Century indifference to design in an arrangement of flowers was customary. Flowers were placed in a container that held water, and that was all. Later, displaying the biggest and the best in flowers became an underlying interest, and a certain pomposity demanded that even the stem of a rose be extremely long. Maybe this trend led to the discovery that certain plants had distinct habits and associations. A beginning awareness of distinct characteristics was strengthened by the introduction of Oriental design in the early 1930s. This sparse, linear method of organizing plant material clashed decidedly with the concept that flowers should be grouped in masses. This new kind of enjoyment, simplicity with an added spice of Oriental symbolism, became greatly acceptable to many people. Thus began a genteel tug of war between the customary, and this newly introduced style.

In the early years, interested people were not yet clear as to whether flower arrangement should be a fashionable fad for the somewhat idle rich, or a hobby of sorts, or perhaps the seed bud for the development of an enduring new cultural asset: a truly popular and creative artistic endeavor! The pendulum swung wildly back and forth. The doors of artistic development in this field opened, and then closed again when conformity became a means of measuring accomplishment. Soon flower arrangers were composing by rote, stiffly and in repetitious patterns of previously executed styles.

All the same, progress was quietly on the march. Flowers were studied: their names, habits and habitats became of great interest. Knowledge of their cultural needs spurred interest in horticulture, botany and conservation. Conditioning for the prolonging of their brief freshness became important and opened a path for commercial enterprise. On a broad scale, the evolution of a sweeping American cultural development was underway. We had taken hold of a flower, and by touching one part of it, were compelled to hold on to many other parts. Even then arrangers touched the elements of design: the smooth-skinned stem lines, the perfect form of the open or budding flower, the wondrously translucent color of the petals, their dewy textures, and the crisp pattern of leaf and stem. They breathed in the aroma from the kingdom of plants, becoming conscious of these treasures. The thirst for more and deeper knowledge and understanding was under way.

The study of color, its power and its discipline, became absorbing and led in many surprising directions. The chiaroscuro depiction of light and dark, intensity, the myriad values of the different hues, all were studied. Color pigments are manufactured by the plants; their luminosity and rainbow translucency encapsulate qualities of the spectrum. The high threshold of physics and optics spreads open. So often the pose of a plant is characteristic, and without seeing its detail, we can identify it from afar. The knowledge of growth and its characteristics, or its deviations, opens endless possibilities which are limited only by the mechanics of execution. Imagination should have a field day.

The pendulum did not swing with excitement, however. It stood still. The newly found knowledge was absorbed, analyzed, neatly categorized and pigeonholed. Conformity to the respective cubbyholes became a requirement, and certain assets were expected to be present in every flower arrangement. Color and design were overly-organized qualities that soon made the arrangement look trite and stilted. But to any unregimented American designer, an individual mental approach is a necessary democratic privilege. Indeed, to the skilled arranger, the idea and actual execution by a disciplined plan which uses the elemental treasures of plant material becomes the outstanding satisfaction. Thus, the pendulum swung again.

Each of the general principles of art—the establishment of visual and physical balance, the measurement of good proportion, the fine relationship of the size of objects as well as their relationship to each other, the use and awareness of space—all now became fundamental tools of the arranger. The knowledge of rhythmic, repetitious impact, of transitory thresholds, and of swelling and ebbing size relationships was commonplace. To lift harmonies to greater vibrancy, sharp, contrasting accents or dominant impacts were utilized with great skill. Indeed, a whole vocabulary of specific words came into being for judges who evaluate the accomplishments of others.

Studies of Oriental styles of design added realization of the value of the three-dimensional touch. It was only another step into the understanding of a need for attention to the relationship of the volume of plant material to the volume of involved space. Soon the doors burst wide open from the impetus of self-expression. The search for beauty aimed ever higher in this particular medium, which is so different from painting, sculpture, music or poetry, and yet, so very close to each of them. Today, flower arranging has become a means of self-expression in our world and in our time. It evolves clearly into one of the most satisfying and appealing pleasures, a constant stimulus to our imaginations.

Simplicity of expression, harmony, and suitability for the medium and its functional effect are certainly the same qualities inherent in all fine arrangements of the past. But today, expressiveness identifies the imaginative arranger to whom the creation of beauty is both a freedom and a discipline, and at the same time provides opportunity and challenge. Fundamentally, the importance of an arrangement has changed from a decorative effect to a creative expression of ideas and thoughts about beauty, with a direct and personal approach to the beholder.

The physical construction of an arrangement has no strings attached. Without rigidity, we are allowed to compose on a larger and wider scale within the limits of good taste. In this new freedom, the need for strict discipline is just as fundamental as ever. So is a thorough, completely assimilated knowledge of all conceivable tools of design, and a knowledge of the medium: *plant material*. Whether we work in recognized harmonies or in harmonic discords, whether we work with polychromatic or achromatic materials, our work is to record our creative expression of the moment in relation to our subject. We may do this by the use of massive amounts of materials, or by great simplicity of line in relation to space. We may be excited about color and use one or several well-known harmonies, with complete understanding of their impact.

Figure 1.
A bold modern design that shows definite Oriental influence.

The time in which we live allows us completely new concepts of line and pattern. Placement in space of angles and curves, straight planes or warped lines, parallels and abstract geometric patterns, used singly or combined with realistic growth patterns, give the gifted arranger unending excitement and satisfaction. The fun of adventure and the use of an uninhibited capacity for imagination are the exciting and constructive happenings of today. Courage to walk alone and a bit off the beaten path is the requirement if one is aiming to catch this end of a sparkling rainbow!

Figure 2.

Another design showing strong Oriental influence.

The Nature of Art

Certain art term definitions are applied to painting and sculpture. Since we consider floral art a visual art, it, too, falls into this category. Think of flower arranging whenever you read these definitions, and apply them to our medium.

Definitions

Abstract, abstraction: Terms given to forms created by the artist, but usually derived from objects actually observed or experienced. Abstraction usually involves a simplification and/or rearrangement of natural objects to meet needs of artistic organization or expression. Sometimes there is so little resemblance to the original object that the shapes seem to have no relationship to anything experienced in the natural environment.

Academic: A term applied to any kind of art that stresses the use of accepted rules for technique and form organization. It represents the exact opposite of the original approach, and often results in a vital, individual style of expression.

Content: The essential significance or aesthetic value of an art form. *Content* refers to the sensory, psychological or emotional properties that we tend to feel in a work of art, as opposed to the perception of mere descriptive aspects.

Craftsmanship: Aptitude, skill or manual dexterity in the use of tools and materials.

Figure 3.
Striking in its simplicity, this design emphasizes the strength of line.

Design: A framework or scheme of pictorial construction on which artists base the formal organization of their total work. In a broader sense, design may be considered synonymous with the term *form*.

Form: The arbitrary organization or inventive arrangement of all the visual elements, according to principles that will develop an organic unity in the total work of art.

Media, mediums: The materials and tools used by the artist to create the visual elements perceived by the viewer of the work of art (in our case this is plant materials).

Figure 4.

Plant materials are used in their natural forms, with no abstraction, to create a dramatic design with tremendous visual appeal.

Naturalism: The approach to art in which all forms used by the artist are essentially a descriptive representation of things visually experienced. True *naturalism* contains no interpretation introduced by the artist for expressive purposes. The complete recording of the visual effects of nature is a physical impossibility, and naturalistic style thus becomes a matter of degree.

Nonobjective: An approach to art in which the visual signs are entirely imaginative and not derived from anything ever seen by the artist. The shapes, their organization and their treatment by the artist are not associated by the observer with any previously experienced natural form.

Optical perception: A way of seeing in which the mind seems to have no other function than the natural one of providing the physical sensation of recognition of form. *Conceptual perception,* on the other hand, refers to the artist's imagination and creative vision.

Realism: A form of expression that retains the basic impression of visual reality but, in addition, attempts to relate and interpret the universal meanings that lie underneath the surface appearance of natural form.

Representational: A manner of expression by the artist in which the subject matter is presented through the visual elements so the observer is reminded of actual forms.

Style: The specific artistic character and dominant form trends noted in certain art movements or during specific periods of history. *Style* may also mean artists' expressive use of the media to give their works individual character.

Subject matter: This term in a descriptive style of art refers to the persons or things represented, as well as the artist's experiences, that serve as inspiration. In abstract or nonobjective forms of art, *subject matter* refers merely to the basic character of all the visual signs employed by the artist. In this case, *subject matter* has little to do with anything experienced in the natural environment.

Technique: The manner and skill with which artists employ their tools and materials to achieve a predetermined expressive effect. The ways of using the media can have an effect on the aesthetic quality of an artist's total concept.

Art: the Language of Visual Signs

Art has meant different things to different people at different times. The term as we use it today probably is derived from the Renaissance words *arti* and *arte*. *Arti* was the designation for the craft guilds of the 14th, 15th and 16th Centuries to which the artists were closely tied by the traditions of their calling. *Arte,* the word for craftsmanship, implied a knowledge of materials used by the artist, such as the chemical nature of pigments and their interaction with one another, as well as the grounds to which a painter applied those pigments. *Arte,* or craftsmanship, also implied skillful handling of those materials in the sense of producing images more or less like those of nature. Art in the Renaissance thus served both as a technical and an interpretive record of human experience. It has continued to fulfill this function down to the present time, although less meaningfully at some times than at others. In the 19th

Century, emphasis was often placed on the technical aspects of art, but in the hands of the greatest masters it always remained interpretive.

Art always deals with visual signs to convey ideas, moods or generalized emotional experiences. It may be called "the language of visual signs." Unlike the language of words, however, art is not meant to be informative. Information is the province of symbols, as in the words of literature or the numbers of mathematics. Sometimes in the interpretation of ideas or moods, the artist may employ visual symbols, but the meaning of such symbols is embodied in the forms or images that the artist creates, just as the ideas, moods or experiences the artist conveys.

Since art is not intended to convey facts or information, the appreciation of art may be enhanced when the observer attempts to grasp the meaning of works of art through intuition or instinct. Although observers may realize that the language of words and that of visual signs as used in art are disparate, they may not recognize the varied problems that arise in understanding and explaining art. The limitations of the printed or spoken word in fully explaining art must be accepted as the natural inability of one medium to replace another. These words were never truer than in our case, where plant materials are used as our medium. And when we go beyond the traditional aspects of flower arranging, we are then opening our art to the volume of knowledge that embellishes all art forms. It is difficult, with our limited knowledge of other arts, to express ourselves to the fullest.

We have all felt the frustration that accompanies our attempt to describe a moving experience to a friend. We are soon convinced that the only description lies in the experience itself. Nonetheless, for education toward a better understanding of art, the medium of words has to be used in an attempt to explain the nature of art and the ideas presented by the works of art. Unfortunately, the most moving experiences are usually those that are least expressible, no matter how much we may wish to share them. The sensations of experience vary according to the senses that are stimulated, and since certain major divisions of art developed around each of these senses, we may assume that certain qualities exist that make these means separate, as well as unique.

The lay person often assumes that an artwork should be recognizable and should tell a story in a visually descriptive manner. Some great works of art in the past have often told stories, but artists are under no obligation to narrate, since narration is not directly a part of their medium. Even when artists have chosen to narrate, their pictorial story may be visualized in many ways, due to the nature of an artistically expressed form. In the 19th Century, when the influence of poetry and prose reached its zenith, art often became a handmaiden of literature and, aided by science, attempted factual interpretation of romantic and allegorical writing. There was marked abandonment of form as an expressive agent in its own right, while the favored subject matter was saturated with emotion and sentimentality. The role of art became one of narration and description, as though one attempted to give a feeling of battle by counting the troops and weapons, or tried to express mother-love by taking an inventory of the nursery equipment. In short, artists had de-emphasized the essential ingredients of art and made it a second-rate translator of other media.

Art must, in its way, narrate and describe to some degree, for it is a medium developed out of our need for a particular type of communication. However, art is at its best when its form is communicated directly, with subject matter and symbols playing subordinate roles. The mechanics of art reception tend to be quite different for the most part from those of other media. For example, painting and sculptures do not usually flow in time (Alexander Calder proved the exception with his Mobiles), nor do they involve physical anticipation, as in turning the pages of a book or listening for the next measure of music. The complete unity of a painting registers in a moment. This is also very true of a creative flower arrangement. The

Figure 5.

A pleasing all-green design has elements of the traditional, but organization of materials shows a beginning toward the more creative arrangement of components.

totality of the work can be taken in with one hard look, although this is hardly the recommended procedure for real appreciation. Hence painting and sculpture, graphic processes like drawings, printmaking as well as floral design, do not lend themselves wholeheartedly to the recitation of action in sequence form as does literature, which is unfolding in its presentation. Narration is more properly a by-product of the artist's search.

If you have thought "floral design" throughout the above, then you will have a more complete understanding of the theory of the nature of art: what it is, how we are to create it, and better still, how we evaluate it as a true art form. In fact, it is the greatest of all visual arts, because the medium is always new, exciting and ever changing as nature itself develops through the process of plant growth and development. It then becomes our duty as designers to select and unite these chosen forms of nature into works of art called floral designs.

Figure 6.

An even more creative placement of materials is shown in this design, which includes crossing lines as well as other strongly vertical and horizontal placements.

How Art-Isms Influence Creative Ability

Realism: Fidelity to natural appearances without slavish attention to minute details. As a movement, it goes back to Gustave Courbet and Claude Manet in the 1850s, and culminates in Impressionism. In general, it is the depiction of human figures, real objects, or scenes as they appear in nature, without distortion or stylization. The realistic flower arranger is concerned with recreating nature as we see it, with little imagination in creating the unseen elements. A totally recognizable effort is achieved. We can list the Traditional Mass design lovers in this category because their total involvement with color and form is an expression of total beauty. Also in this list will fall those who are involved with Ikebana (the art of Japanese flower arrangement).

Romanticism: The artist's recording of picturesque scenes, abnormal faces and exciting events, with individualism in appearance and approach. It is emotional in contemplation of subject matter, a devotion to strange examples, and a presentation made exciting by virtue of its movement and color. Magnificence and grandeur are aims, using fresh coloring and vibrating light. This was the forerunner of Impressionism. The artist painting in this vein is fleeing a place and time that has little meaning for him.

The creative Romantic designer will become more involved with subject matter than total reproduction of mirror images of the subject. The picturesque theory will be deepened if and when they seek out the unseen forces in their expressions. However, the masses of designers fall into this category, and their works become in most cases a decorative form of expression. To recreate nature as it is, indeed, takes time and effort, and a certain amount of creativity will pull the design into life as one of beauty and charm. This has happened with the creative Japanese arrangers of today, as they have combined eastern and western cultures into a new form of Ikebana. The Romanticists also involve emotional qualities of expression in the designs that are decorative in concept, but depict birthdays, weddings, holidays, etc. A clever artist may reflect romantic theory and character, but then develop it into a creative expression.

Impressionism: The first great modern art movement. The Impressionists broke away from the traditional technique of continuous brush strokes, from the representation of clearly outlined objects, and from preconceived notions of the color that things have in nature. They sought instead to break up light into its component parts and to render its ephemeral play on various surfaces. To achieve their effects, they worked in a succession of discontinued strokes of color, which were to be combined by the eye.

Although Impressionist paintings did not conform to traditional ideas of how things should be depicted, they were in fact attempts to observe nature as it really is and to transmit it to canvas. Bright colors in a high key were characteristic of Impressionist work. This is a method of losing forms in a tissue of atmospheric variation. A visual observation is taken as a starting point, and color is added out of the imagination in order to lose visual forms, resulting in an overall architectural form. Plastic organization stresses volumes that induce airy movement, but solid foundations involve volume and space, plane and texture of dark-light and colors. These reduce the solid qualities of an object and minimize the role of line. Contours are vaguely sketched. Colors are laid on in flat areas, but harmony is introduced by matching certain sets of hues. Broken color is employed for overall effect.

The first step toward abstraction is, thus, made by the Impressionism artist. The design begins to lose total image and takes on an individual impression of the subject matter. The subject is there, but it becomes more vague in formation. Transparency is induced to hide the subject, and total identity is lost. The spirit of the subject is induced to the point that some parts of the design may become more important than others. Individual expression becomes evident, and what impresses one may not impress another, so the individual aspect of modern art is born.

This form of art is totally individualistic, and induces an inner spirit that had not existed before. The true balance then becomes half realistic and half impressionistic in feeling. The viewer becomes involved for the first time, as study and evaluation are important in order to understand the artist's intent. Expressive or interpretive floral designs in theory should take on another character with Impressionism. The process of Creativity involves the designer in re-creating the subject, not in total traditional reproduction, but in a manner that expresses the artist's own individual approach to the subject matter.

Expressionism: A concept in painting in which traditional adherence to canons of realism and proportion is overridden by the intensity of the artist's emotions, resulting in distortion of line, shape and color. Whereas the Impressionists were concerned with rendering nature in a new and more valid way, painters such as Les Fauves and Vincent Van Gogh considered their emotions to be as important as their subject matter. Expressionism was brought to the status of a full and vigorous movement by the artists of Germany during the first quarter of the 20th Century, especially by the Brucke, Blue Reiter and Neue Sachlichkeit groups.

Like much of modern art, Expressionism owes a great deal to the impact of African sculpture on Europe in the decade preceding World War I. The art was represented by voluminous figures placed solidly in space. Contrast was emphasized and exaggerated. Broad, drastically simplified colorful canvas served as "stars" of a composition. A personal feeling was maintained. Formal design and plastic organization were disregarded for effect. Backgrounds were usually eliminated. Pictorial symbolism was derived from passion or emotional frenzy. Artists wanted to express the soul through inwardly conceived images. A loose, careless type of painting was employed to reveal inner truth and character, often psychologically revealing. These works often penetrate the outward shell of reality.

Expressionism is closely related to pure abstraction and is developed into artistic emotion. It is entirely original in form, without being representational in its expression. The artist's feeling is expressed by the subject matter. Expressionism became even more personal and individual than any art form prior to its development, because of its inner feelings. All surface qualities fade away, and bold forceful forms advance to express an idea. It becomes a game of psychology as artists analyze a subject more thoroughly in their expressions.

In flower arranging, a card is suggested to inform the judge and viewing public to what has been used and why it was handled as it was in the design. Plant materials are no longer viewed as solely plant materials, but become line, form, color and texture to express the idea of the artist. This theory is difficult to understand because this inner theory does not often agree with a Realistic or Romantic approach to the subject matter.

Cubism: The Cubist style had three stages of development: *Facet Cubism*, in which the artist started to separate objects of figures into definite, geometrical elements or facets, while placing them in a composition (which still showed the influence of Paul Cézanne); *Analytical Cubism*, in which objects were increasingly broken down and analyzed through such means as simultaneous rendition and the presentation of several aspects of an object; and *Synthetic Cubism*, in which the artist was further liberated from traditional reality, appearance and illusion.

However, a display of cubistic forms of all dimensions can be exciting if interesting color contrast is used. Also, space volume becomes an inner force to be dealt with; the placement of forms with overlapping planes creates depth that otherwise may have been not that exciting. Large areas should be used for Cubistic designs, as space volume is needed to activate these designs. The smaller the design, the less force is present as the space area is greatly reduced. The most common designs using plant materials are those where the designer has bent straight line materials into a series of geometric forms to create a feeling of construction, to which other plant materials have then been added.

Surrealism: An art movement of the 1920s and later. Surrealist artists attempted to give free reign to the subconscious as a source of creativity, and liberated pictorial ideas from their traditional associations. As a successor to Dada, Surrealism is characterized by some of its techniques, such as the employment of the found-object. Artists who participated in both of these movements included Max Ernst, Jean Arp and Francis Picabia. Abstract Surrealism was practiced by the painter Joan Miró. Other aspects of Surrealist art are the juxtaposition of unexpected objects or themes in an atmosphere of fantasy having a pervasive dreamlike quality. Salvador Dali and Giorgia de Chirico were among the most important creators of the haunting, irrational, occasionally repellent dream world of Surrealistic art.

Beauty, in the Greek or Renaissance sense, is not the aim of abstract theory. Between beauty of expression and power of expression there is a difference in function. The first aim is pleasing the senses; the second has a spiritual vitality that may be more moving, and goes much deeper than the senses. Because a work of art does not aim at reproducing natural appearances, it is not, therefore, an escape from life, but may be a penetration into reality: an expression of the significance of life, a stimulation to greater effort in living.

From the analysis of the art *"-isms"*, perhaps we can find the vein in which we work with flowers. Each *"-ism"*, when studied, will reveal the strong character of many of our modern art forms. A person can't work in all fields of *"-isms"*, so choose those you enjoy most and excel in, then develop them into your own art expressions.

Figure 7.
A rhythmically pleasing design, with great aesthetic appeal. Bold forms are arranged in a fairly traditional manner, using radial placement of materials.

CHAPTER TWO

The Essence of Creativity

Style is an individualistic manner of creating. It is a personal interpretation of design. Sometimes a style is so fresh, so dynamic, that others are inspired to adopt it. When its popularity becomes general, it is considered the prevailing style of a period. If what we now call "creative" stands the test of time, it will take its place along with traditional styles and be considered representative of the 20th century and beyond. If it is just the fad of the day, it will die and be forgotten.

In all the arts, we learn from the past, but we try to create for the future. Creative flower arrangement is characterized by great variety. European styles have been revitalized and adapted to new techniques. The art, as practiced in China and Japan, shows its influence in the importance we place on pure line, and the beauty we achieve through simplicity and naturalness. Oriental arrangements have a special quality of life and growth, and no element appears to be unnatural or distorted in order to carry out the overall design. We, too, try to suggest the growth pattern of our material, but our work bears the stamp of a new era. While we may feel nostalgic for the past, the tempo of the electronic age demands something entirely new in the way of design.

This is an age of unrivaled scientific discovery, the most crucial era yet known to man. As the modern miracles of communication herald the wonders of their research, we begin to see a design in our expanding universe, learn to interpret its laws, and use them for our own purpose. Art, as well as science, is progressing along new lines with the fresh stimulus of added knowledge. As nonessentials are stripped away, pure design stands out with new vigor and boldness.

"Streamlined" is a word that is much used and often abused, but it accurately describes the design of the present day. It is reflected in our architecture, furniture, cars and planes. Artists are sensitive to their environment. They are driven by a strong compulsion to find some visual form to interpret the spirit of their era. Abstract art may not appeal to you, but it does represent a new way of communicating an idea that the artist considers important. The abstract artist casts aside liberal translation and depends upon purity of line, color and texture to express a thought or emotion. We are more familiar with the art of abstraction than we may think. We practice abstraction when we make a flower arrangement, for we take the flower out of its natural setting to use the force and power of its color, form and line as a means of self-expression. This is not an attempt to distort the truth, but a challenge to present it in a new form so that its effect is unmistakable.

Each arrangement should bear a "signature," the mark of its creator made evident by a personal technique. New approaches and fresh points of view stimulate imagination and keep us out of the rut of imitation, which eventually becomes the grave of ingenuity. When you can trust your instincts to cut through restraints and work in the full sunshine of inspiration, you will put your personal signature on everything you do. Flower arrangement qualifies as a fine art only when it becomes a medium for self-expression.

The greatest challenge to the modern designer is the interpretive arrangement, which tells a story, creates a mood, or translates an idea into visual form. To be understood by others, the idea must be dramatic and bold, and expressed with sincerity. If we are given the theme "A June Day" to interpret it may bring to mind a particular day, when the beauty of June was typified for us by the daisies we picked in a field. We may remember lines from a well-loved poem, or a picture that caught the quality of June sunlight.

When we call upon the images in our minds and all the information we have gathered by means of careful research, inspiration will come with surprising rightness. The next step in creating an interpretive design is to find materials that effectively reveal our thought. We have endowed many inanimate objects with symbolic meaning, and occasionally we find a place for them in a composition. But there are other ways to make a thought visible. The character of lines, their placements and associations have a definite psychological effect. Color makes a vigorous impact that is invaluable in expressing a mood. Unusual forms and interesting textures are the contemporary arranger's greatest aid to expression.

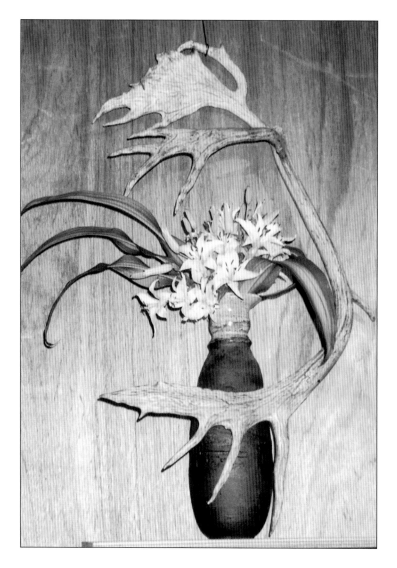

Figure 8.

A very unusual form, represented by the dramatic antlers, inspires a bold and dynamic design. White lilies with brilliant red pollen provide color and textural interest.

Figure 9.
The large rhythmic philodendron leaf, placed high in the design, provides dynamic impact. Clusters of small pine cones attached at intervals to the container add additional textural interest, as do the pale yellow proteas.

The idea or thought must be fused with an appropriate form that will allow you to transfer your deeply-felt emotion and to capture and translate the inner spirit. We are told that the key to this symbolic expression is found in the body itself, for the outer attitude reflects the inner spirit. Study the attitude of the body as it expresses joy, anger, tranquillity, sorrow. Without speaking a word, a man with the gift of pantomime can tell a complete story. In the same way, the forms and lines of an arrangement can be made to express a mood. If you wish to suggest sorrow, you recognize the drooping, dejected attitude that the body unconsciously assumes when you are sad. Use this form as an outline or pattern for your design. But form is not enough. You know when the color blue is used to excess, with the intensity dulled and the value darkened, the observer experiences a wave of sadness. Since vitality and meaning of lines are lost in masses of materials, let restraint guide you in establishing strong, unconfused lines.

Figure 10. *(Left)*
Bold palm spathes, swirling garlands of twisted vines and heavily textured banksias are used in a design in which interest is equated throughout.

Figure 11. *(Opposite)*
Varying intervals and shapes of enclosed spaces, created by the weathered wood and the container, add interest to this creative design. A large leaf is trimmed into a more tailored form, and the two furry banksias provide needed contrast through texture and form.

We are breaking away from slavish acceptance of all that has been done before, and are using the elements of design in a new and bold way. Creative arrangements, for example, are liberated from the precision of set geometric patterns. Less attention is given to a focal point or area of acceleration. Because a designer may end a line with a bold form, we say a "rule" has been broken —and so it has, but not the principles of design. Greater understanding of art principles is required to work with freer forms. It is not license to ignore laws that have stood the test of time, but is liberty to translate what we know into what we do.

An important characteristic of creative design is its conscious use of space. Space is not a neglected area, but a rest from the activity of solid placements. It moves in and out of the structural planes and fills each unoccupied area. Creative arrangements have charm, beauty and interest of contour from any angle. Strength of contrast is emphasized, and little or no transitional material is used. The goal is distinction, not delicate prettiness. These have the vitality and boldness of the age they represent. Creative arrangements are fastidious and neat, requiring technical perfection and the efficient use of necessary mechanical aids. Their inspiration may come from far places, as do many of the materials in use today, but to qualify as a creative arrangement, the elements of our design must be made to reflect the spirit of our own era.

Figure 12.

An unusual container holds a graceful, curved piece of weathered wood, whose line is complemented on the opposite side by placement of clipped palm and brilliant pink proteas. Placement of one protea at the top of the wood continues the rhythmic flow in a creative manner.

Creative Freedom

In freedom of creativity, we are granted liberties that make our work gratifying, including the following:

- To choose and use unusual containers with multiple openings.

- To be able to make our own creative containers out of "found" materials like junk, pieces of metal, unusual wood forms, plastics, etc.

- To combine common garden or roadside materials with exotic tropical materials from other countries (granted to us by modern means of transportation).

- To write flower show schedules that will reflect imaginative concepts in staging that will showcase our designs creatively.

- To choose and use any combination of components in our designs—wood, metal, plastic, glass—with plant materials and anything else conceivable that inspires us to use it.

- To no longer be confined to small designs allows our designs to soar into space, incorporate space, and for the first time use space as a positive force within our creations.

- To place our plant material out of water, upside down or in any manner needed to "design."

- To use the expressive qualities of plant material to convey our ideas on any subject.

- To discard traditional mechanics and learn to balance, wedge and hold our plant materials in place in innovative ways.

- To be able to see beauty in a single leaf, flower or line.

These are only a few of our new freedoms found in Creativity. If you will think about it, you may add many more things to this list. A world of flowers without creativity: how dull it would be. Our flight into this exciting world has been a rough one, and we must never turn our controls over to those who do not understand our world, lest we return to a more academic way with flowers. Our followers have proven their ability and knowledge in many ways; our leading exhibitions (flower shows, museum shows, etc.) are filled with new, exciting concepts that attract viewers by being departures from the norm. They are dynamic, forceful symbols of today's way with flowers. A creative approach will always be refreshing and cause comment.

The Search

The joy of a search is evident within all of us when we explore nature and man's environment for unthought-of-materials and components with which to express our creative efforts. It is in this search that we find satisfaction and gratitude for our means of expression. The seeing eye can uncover many "found," beautiful and interesting forms to which the creative process can be applied. A search is always a must, because it is not often that these items are handed to us on a silver platter. A little inconvenience can be most rewarding later when we use our "found" items in creative designs.

Figure 13. *(Left)*
A spiraling piece
of rope establishes
the dominant
rhythmic line of
this design. Orange
lilies contribute
contrast in form
and color.

Figure 14. *(Opposite)*
Two pieces of fasciated
asparagus provide
beautiful rhythmic line,
as well as interesting
texture. Placement of
two groups of yellow
lilies creates two areas
of interest.

Most of our sought-for items lie hidden and can be found in most unusual places. Field trips with fellow arrangers, a trip into the woods, along lake or river shores, or even a trek along a railroad track can be rewarding. Nature, with man's help (through insecticide spray, etc.), can produce natural forms that have been distorted perfectly for our designs. Always wear appropriate clothing—boots, jeans, gloves—and be sure to take proper cutting materials: saw, clippers, pruners and the like. Explore as you search. Turn over pieces of wood to find a surprisingly lovely textural pattern underneath. Cut what you like, with additional pruning upon arrival at home. Take a van or truck because a successful search will bring rewarding results.

In traveling, avoid always taking the interstate; back roads, untraveled by many, can reward the creative person greatly. Check junk yards for unusual auto parts or second-hand stores for rewarding forms of interest. The truly creative soul will continue to select and reject materials in this never ending search of creativity.

Creative People

Creative people do at least seven things well:

1. They challenge assumptions.
2. They recognize patterns.
3. They see in new ways.
4. They make connections.
5. They take risks.
6. They maximize chances.
7. They construct networks of people for exchange of ideas, perceptions, questions and encouragement.

Challenging Assumptions: People once assumed that the earth was flat, that the sun revolved around the earth and that evil spirits caused diseases. The thinkers who challenged these assumptions were scorned, imprisoned and despised by their contemporaries. When we accept without questioning, we may not see alternatives open to us. Children, for example, often ask "WHY?" in questioning things that adults take for granted. Albert Einstein valued this childlike curiosity as the work of the creative spirit, and many of our, scientists and inventors practice this independence of thought.

Recognizing Patterns: Recognizing patterns is perceiving significant similarities or differences in ideas, events or physical phenomena. In searching for patterns, we attempt to give form to the world. Detecting patterns in the unknown is a way of creating order out of chaos. Patterns can be found in nearly everything. Sigmund Freud, for example, observed patterns of human behavior in trying to understand the human psyche. Astronomers watch the sky to find patterns of motion that help us understand the universe. Gregor Mendel, crossbreeding peas in a monastery garden, observed patterns that led to a new perception about heredity. Patterns in the ocean floor led scientists to a new understanding of how the earth is constantly changing.

Figure 15.
Swirling wisteria vines are complemented by "Stargazer" lilies and torch ginger in a design incorporating much visual movement.

Seeing in New Ways: Seeing in new ways involves more than just sight; it is the essence of imagination. Unusual, interesting forms stir the imagination of each individual viewer. Wood forms found along shorelines of bodies of water, creek banks or in wooded areas appear to become distorted forms found in a vivid imagination of different mirror images of realistic forms. We see animals, reptiles and birds because of our association through nature.

Making Connections: Making connections can be like the moment in a mystery story when the author suddenly allows the link between two episodes or characters to become apparent. For example, Edward Jenner noticed that smallpox never afflicted milkmaids. By making the connection that the milkmaids became immune by being exposed to the milder disease of cowpox, he derived the principle of vaccination. Guttenberg took the idea of woodblock printing, used for playing cards and pictures, and thought of making blocks of letters of the alphabet. The result was movable type. "Similarity is not a thing offered on a plate," said Arthur Koestler, author of *Darkness at Noon*. "It is a relationship established in the mind."

Taking Risks: Creative people take risks and try long-shot ideas. Columbus, Drake, Magel-lan and other explorers took fearful risks when they set out on long voyages into the unknown seas. Besides the dangers from storms, sickness and other potential misfortunes, they

Figure 16.

Accentuated horizontal lines of New Zealand flax and weathered yucca stems are
balanced by a grouping of additional weathered wood, loops of flax and strelitzia flowers.

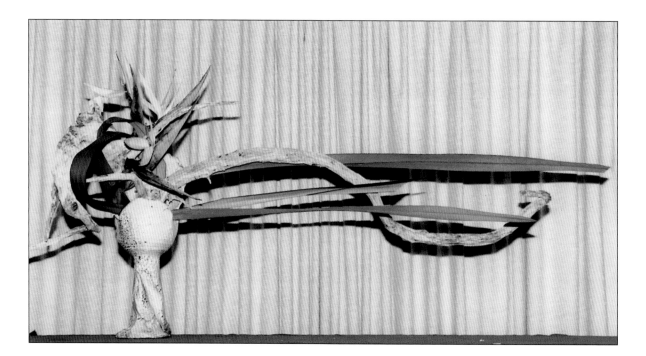

also believed they risked encounters with sea monsters and supernatural powers. Alexander Graham Bell risked new ventures even after his success with the telephone. Some, such as the iron lung, worked. Others, like the photophone, did not.

Using Chance: "Chance favors only the prepared mind," said Louis Pasteur. Using chance is something the creative person learns to do. Jackson Pollock used chance in painting his canvasses, and John Cage used chance in composing musical scores. Charles Goodyear discovered the process of vulcanizing rubber by chance. He had been experimenting with various chemicals, trying to make raw rubber usable. But it wasn't until he accidentally dropped some raw rubber onto a hot stove that he realized heat was the solution to the problem.

Constructing Networks: While creativity is an intensely individual phenomenon, forming associations between people for the exchange of ideas is extraordinarily useful for the creative person. In Paris in the 1920s, an international set of artists and writers gathered and were nourished by each other's work: Pablo Picasso, Ernest Hemingway, F. Scott Fitzgerald, James Joyce, Igor Stravinsky and Gertrude Stein. The work of scientists is also shared worldwide. We can compare these groups with our Judges' Councils, Flower Arranging Guilds and study groups. "A net is stronger than its separate strands." The world of creativity is in dire need of those who are willing to accept the challenge. Try it! You will like it! A word of warning to help those who are starting the venture with a background of traditional thoughts and rules: a well-learned and skillfully executed design may be habit forming. It may, and can be, a complete bore. Fitting your plant material media into a "formula" design is good training and exercise, but the arranger should not feel too comfortable with a design, especially when it becomes a constant repetition, like that of a Hogarth line or a Triangular Mass, that is repeated over and over. Each design should become a new adventure, a magnificent journey into a new world through your excitement and pleasure in arranging in a new way.

Identifying the Creative Design

The most outstanding characteristic of the Creative Design is BOLDNESS . . .

. . . boldness in design, color and materials, containers and accessories. Boldness is best expressed by the use of three or fewer kinds of plant material and three or fewer hues. The design must be free from confusing detail. Exotic flowers, unusual combinations of flowers, foliage and fruits and/or vegetables, do much to promote the awareness of boldness. Unusual wood forms, containers and accessories are helpful.

A creative design must be a self-contained whole, and everything about it,
even the apparently unrelated, must be fused . . .

It must have design, color and emotive spiritual coordination. It may appear chaotic, but to be a successful top award winner, there must be a subtle resolution of the chaos. One must feel through analysis that nothing can be deleted, and that nothing more can be added.

Compositionally the work must be alive and dynamic, not static . . .

If static, no matter how superficially interesting, it easily falls into a branch of decoration, which has its own less exacting criteria. Static unity and static harmony are not elements of great art, although the uninformed are often deceived by them. Many good modern designs are rendered dynamic and self-illuminated through strategic color tensions. We also find some contemporary works sufficiently dynamic, so that they appear to participate in surrounding space. A design, in order to be dynamic, must not only enliven but must control space. This does not mean that all spaces must be filled. On the contrary, unused areas or quiet intervals may be strong parts of a composition.

There must be imaginative, emotional and sensory content . . .

In other words, the mind, spirit, intuition and feeling of the artist must be transferred to and infused into the arrangement, giving it a soul that can live as an independent entity. Technique, materials used and feelings become one; but feelings, spirit and emotion transcend materials and technique. When this happens, the artist is said by the expert to be successfully involved in the finished composition.

Remember: any good arrangement must be an original, fresh, imaginative projection. No artist truly succeeds until he has developed a cosmos that is his own, so clearly that we begin to recognize his work by it. Some artists, for a lack of creative drive, spend their entire life arranging patterns in the styles of others, even in the styles of past centuries. And while their work may be highly expressive and decorative, satisfactory to their own egos, they cannot reach a great, top position. Their enthusiastic and often excellent works flood our shows, but wise and knowledgeable viewers and judges quickly recognize the un-original. Great artists will admit sources, but they try to transcend them completely with their own cosmos.

Great art is the result of dedication to inner creative forces, ideas and intuition. It is free in spirit and knows very little compromise. Although we constantly talk about the necessity of absolute freedom of expression in our creative art, actually a dedicated artist finds himself in one of the tightest psychical traps man has ever invented, because he is in a painful state of self-discipline of his restless inner creative spirit.

The solution lies then in Beauty and Taste. Many times a great work of art will appear ugly to those with limited or too literal romantic standards of beauty and taste. Many people were educated to believe in only a romantic pleasure in art. Thus, the sense of the infinite completely escapes them. An American taken by an Oriental to see an oddly shaped bronze object, quite ancient, said, "How ugly." The Oriental replied, "Ah yes, how ugly, but what a great work of art." We Westerners accept a painting of Christ nailed on a cross because of the symbolism; but it might possibly be thought ugly to some non-Christians. The dictionary defines ugly as "the opposite of beautiful," but in art we must modify this definition. Benedetto Croce, a world authority on aesthetics, said, "Ugly things may be thought of in a beautiful manner and beautiful things in an ugly manner."

Words that we never associate with Creative Design:

Darling . . . Cute . . . Sweet . . . Pretty . . . Crafty . . . Clever

Cunning . . . Brassy . . . Showy . . . Tricky

Although all these words are adjectives and are descriptive in most cases, they are shallow and not meaningful. They are the clichés of the unknowing and are usually said to be polite, without much thought or meaning. Remember that Creative Design has certain appeal to most types of people. Usually the Romanticist-type person never ventures into the realm of the unknown, but stays close to what he or she understands and knows. It takes one with an adventurous spirit to even try Creative Design. There is room for all types of floral art; no one type should be prescribed as being best, or the only way. Each has its own appeal to different individuals.

Words that we associate with creativity:

Artistic . . . Amazing . . . Dramatic . . . Alluring . . . Stimulating

Beautiful . . . Daring . . . Dynamic . . . Masterful . . . Meaningful

Distinctive . . . Original . . . Unusual . . . Sensitive . . . Outstanding

These words are factual, expressive and self-explanatory. Every artist knows he must perfect his medium to the best of his ability. When he is fascinated by a new medium, he must perfect his use of it before allowing the public to view his work.

Are you a creative person? If not, then be considerate of those who are. When you judge or evaluate, remember the following:

- Don't apply old rules to new ideas in design. New designs must have new rules.

- Expose yourself by first looking, then by doing. Attend flower shows and lectures, take lessons, read books and study illustrations.

- Open your mind to something that is new to you. Make an effort to experiment, explore and define.

- Before evaluation as a viewer or as a judge, you should have an appreciation, understanding and a certain compassion for what you are evaluating. Otherwise, how can you have a constructive opinion?

- In judging, leave your personal opinions at home. Judge constructively, not emotionally. Don't attempt to judge any style of arrangement unless you can arrange in this style yourself.

More powerful than the shattering of an atom is the penetration of the human mind—for it is within the human mind that ideas are born, grow and finally burst forth, through communication, toward the betterment of our world.

CHAPTER THREE

Planning and Execution of a Floral Design

Keys to Success: Selectivity, restraint, and good taste

Any good design should have only limited restrictions placed upon it when it is being made. By this, no requirements should be spelled out for the designer to fulfill, such as asking for a certain type of design, type of container, certain combination of plant materials, etc. The artist should have unlimited freedom to create without quantities of restrictions.

Perhaps we tend to tell the arranger what we want in our schedule writing for two reasons:

- *To establish a likeness in all designs in a certain class, in order to evaluate those designs having equal similarities.*

- *To establish variety in our flower shows in order to educate the exhibitors and viewers in a variety of types of specified designs.*

If the above is the purpose, there is argument with this type of education. It, then, becomes a challenge for creative designers to see how well they can conform within the limits of design knowledge. However, if a designer approaches a design assignment with only knowledge of a given title and the required area in which the design is to be placed, the limits of design become more rewarding.

■ **There are certain requirements we must consider when making a design for a FLOWER SHOW.**

1. *Title of class*

2. *Requirements asked for in the schedule* (called "conformance to schedule")

3. *Lighting of exhibit area*

4. *Staging requirements for the class* (niche, pedestal, table area, etc.)

5. *Length of show* (hours exhibit must be on display)

6. *Climatic conditions of show area*

7. *Time of entry*

8. *Time of removal*

■ Considering these requirements, the following things must be taken into careful consideration.

1. *Interpretation of the class title will determine:*
   a. Type of design created
   b. Type of flowers and foliage used
   c. Color of plant materials
   d. Color of background (if needed)

2. *Conformance to schedule requirements will determine:*
   a. Type of design to be created (Traditional or Creative)
   b. Combination of plant materials used (all fresh, fresh and dried or all dried)
   c. How tall or how wide the design may be

3. *Lighting in the exhibit area will govern:*
   a. Color of flowers used
   b. Color of background chosen (if background is used)
   c. Form of line materials selected
   d. Texture of plant materials used
   e. Silhouette of the design created

4. *Staging requirements will govern:*
   a. Height, width and depth of design
   b. If the design is to be free-standing or finished on just one side

5. *Length of show* will determine type of flowers selected for lasting quality, or how often flowers will have to be refreshed.

6. *Time of entry* will determine when the design may be placed in the show area.

7. *Time of removal* will determine when the design is to be removed from the show.

■ **There are certain requirements for making a decorative design for a HOME, CHURCH or PUBLIC BUILDING:**

1. *Decor of surroundings*
2. *Occasion*
3. *Type of container to be used*
4. *Type of flowers to be used*
5. *Color of flowers to be used*
6. *Space available*
7. *Light available*
8. *Type of mechanics*
9. *Work area*

■ Considering these requirements, the following things must be taken into careful consideration:

1. *Decor of surroundings* includes consideration of the period of architecture, furniture and accessories (Accessories are considered the art objects found in a room setting. These should not be removed, but should be complemented by the flower arrangement.)

2. *Occasion* means wedding, reception (what type?), church service, birthday, holiday, etc.

3. *Type of container* most suited for surroundings. Should be in keeping with the period of decor (French, Victorian, Modern, etc.).

4. *Type of flowers* for period of furnishings (formal, informal, rural, festive, etc.)

5. *Color of flowers* and foliage that go well with decor of room

6. *Available space* in which to place the design
   a. This space will determine the size of the design
   b. Available space will determine the form of the design
      (vertical, horizontal, oval, triangular, etc.)

7. Time of day of the occasion will often determine the amount of *light* that is available. Careful consideration would be given to this, as some flowers will sparkle in intense light, while others may fade in color intensity.

8. *Type of mechanics* used will be determined by type of design. A needlepoint holder may be used for line designs or designs with modern character. Oasis or chicken wire may be needed for mass designs requiring quantities of plant materials. Of course, the container will also determine what mechanics are needed.

9. In homes or public buildings a *work area* should be considered, as arranging the flowers in place can be disastrous. Full consideration should be given to the surroundings. One should be neat and considerate of the surrounding furnishings. Be careful with your plant materials, and especially with water. Care should be taken to see that containers do not leak or scratch the surface of furnishings.

The components of design are like characters in a play. Each is chosen for its role, carefully chosen to portray a needed component. *Example:* a gladiolus is chosen for a design because it is typecast for that design. It gives force that is needed to form, color and texture. If another flower were chosen, it would seem out of character. The perfect design is one that has perfect casting. Each component—the container, mechanics, flowers, foliage and accessories, should be chosen for a purpose by you, the producer, to create a well-written play. By selecting the appropriate setting, the perfect lighting and a cast of perfect actors (the flowers, foliage and containers), then a design is completed that will excite and please the viewing playgoer.

It then becomes our task to select or reject the materials we use in our designs. We must, of course, consider what is available and what can be obtained. A good gardener will keep those problems in mind and plant wisely in order to have certain plant materials available. Selectivity will not only guide you in the proper choice of what to use, but also—in that much more difficult aspect of decision—what not to use. Try to be as courageous as the designer who said, "I do wonderful things with leftovers, I throw them away." We all have a tendency to use something just because it is beautiful in itself, when many times we should put it aside rather than spoil a well-considered effect.

In the few statements given above, you will have noticed that there are several things to consider when we start to make a design. However, we, as designers, can always be successful if we carefully select our components, use restraint in the quantities of materials we use, and make sure that whatever we do is governed by good taste, because these are the true keys to success in any design situation.

Figure 17.

A very restrained design contains only the barest essentials to establish line, but form and texture are also emphasized.

Figure 18.

A much more complex design due to the form of the looped and twisted vine, but it is exciting due to selection of compatible components.

Achieving Aesthetic Effect

Any work of art is characterized by unity in design, aesthetic balance, rhythm and harmony. In many works of art, whether music, painting or flower arranging, aesthetic pleasure is the sole purpose. The art medium of music is sound; that of painting is pigment with light; that of flower arranging is plant material. In many flower arrangements no effort is made to arouse the senses. On the other hand, with some works of art, the principle purpose is to evoke ideas and emotions. In the highest form of art, aesthetics is united with a message capable of developing emotional response. "Devotion to true beauty may perhaps be considered as a form of religion, for it leads through sacrifice to lofty attributes of spirit" (Wu Ming Fu).

An artist must know the possibilities and the limitations of the medium in which he works. He must be sensitive to his material. The particular idea a composer may evoke in the mind of a sensitive observer depends not only upon the notes, the pigments or plant material of his medium, but also upon their arrangement in the composition. A pianist striking the same notes may produce either a lullaby or a military march. An orator using a given set of words may, by variations of arrangement, intonation and emphasis, incite his audience either to sympathy or to violence. Similarly, a given lot of plant material may be arranged in different ways that will evoke in the mind of a viewer different emotions and different ideas.

Aesthetic effect created through Line and Mass: The charm of an etching by a master is due to the beauty of lines and spaces, together with the pleasure of suggestion made to the beholder by the picture. The idea is represented by the simplest means, black lines on white paper. But for a successful etching, each line must be placed in proper relationship to the

Figure 19.

Dynamic balance is achieved with two groupings of varied plant materials, each drawing the eye to themselves. The two placements of massed materials combine with the container to draw the eye along a gracefully curving line.

others. The etching without shading is an example of a line design. The boundary lines of the colored areas of many water colors are so indistinct that all forms are indefinite when viewed from a considerable distance. Yet these water color paintings may be highly pleasing because of the beauty of groupings of colored areas. Similarly, a mezzotint engraving or an India ink wash drawing may show no distinct lines and no colors, and yet, the distribution of its light and dark areas may make a fine picture. A design in which areas are more important elements than lines is called a Mass Design. The principal appeal of lines is to the intellect, whereas the appeal of color areas is to the senses and emotions. Most floral arrangements designed by those who appreciate Oriental art are Line Designs.

LINE DESIGN: Created with plant material, Line Designs are founded upon considerations of the silhouette of the design: straight and curved lines, parallel and diverging lines, shapes of spaces between lines. The foundation of a Traditional Design is a group of lines that can be traced all the way from the water surface, which in a sense represents the earth from which the plant material is growing, to the tip of each branch or flower stalk. These radial lines

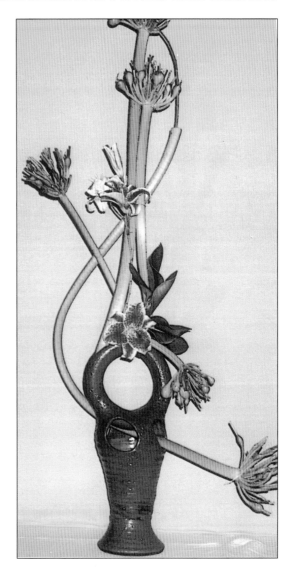

may converge for a certain distance near their origin at the water surface, but for the greater part of their length they should be separated by empty spaces of pleasing shape. The silhouette should have a deeper indented outline of graceful contour.

Although no branch or flower stem is absolutely straight, some are so slightly curved that it is common to call them straight. The zigzag is a very important line in both Oriental and Occidental art. Where the angles are more rounded, the zigzag becomes an undulating line. Many twigs and branches exhibit interesting zigzag lines. Several species of flowers grow in a zigzag placement on flower stalks. Empty spaces are highly important components of a design. When the contours are lines having abstract beauty of their own, they contribute to the pleasing qualities of the arrangement.

Figure 20.

A dramatic design emphasizes freely flowing lines, drawing the eye in a linear path. Strategically placed "Stargazer" lilies provide periodic visual resting points, as well as contrast in color and form.

Figure 21. *(Opposite)*

While the decorative wood and calla lilies establish a strongly vertical line direction, the zigzagged edges of the foliage establish another area of interest within the design.

Figure 22. *(Right)*

A Traditional Mass Design has very pleasing use of compatible forms, colors and textures, combining for a highly decorative effect.

MASS DESIGN: Most paintings by Occidental artists are examples of Mass Designs having beautiful forms, with different areas, hues and tones arranged to exhibit aesthetic balance, rhythm, harmony and unity according to the art principles applied to any design. Flower arrangements constructed as Traditional Mass Designs depend so much on color harmony that a fairly extensive treatment of color sensation is given.

Aesthetic Balance: The state of apparent equilibrium of forms, areas, lines and tones is called aesthetic balance. The condition in which the parts of a design give the beholder the satisfaction of rest is called *static balance*. The simplest type of static balance is attained by arranging the elements of the design symmetrically with respect to a vertical axis through the center of the base of the design. This has been the usual type of balance in religious art throughout the ages. It is still used in many classes of design in Occidental countries, but centuries ago was largely abandoned by Oriental artists in favor of the more difficultly attained, but more satisfying, aesthetic balance produced by asymmetrical placement of elements.

Aesthetic balance in a design may be attained by arranging lines, surfaces and empty spaces of unequal size asymmetrically on opposite sides of the median axis. Each empty space should have its own significance. It is left to the viewer to have the satisfaction of filling it in accordance with his own feelings. A blank space may be more eloquent than superfluous detail.

The appearance of balance also depends upon the distribution of elements according to their tone, whether light or dark. For a symmetrical design, tone balance is brought about by placing the darker elements close to the vertical axis near the base of the design, while the elements of lighter tone are arranged symmetrically with respect to the vertical axis. In an asymmetrical design, tone balance is attained by placing the lighter elements asymmetrically farther from it. In either symmetrical or asymmetrical design, a dark area below a light area will give a feeling of stability.

Figure 23.

Two placements of clipped palm and red gladiolus illustrate aesthetic asymmetrical balance, which is achieved through careful placement of components within the design.

Figure 24.

Careful placement of bunches of equisetum and strelitzia flowers establish the central vertical axis of the symmetrically balanced design, and are balanced by the two cascading asparagus fern (Asparagus Sprengeri) branches on either side.

Symmetrical balance is static, and as lifeless as an Egyptian pyramid. Although it is mechanically satisfying, it is not aesthetically stimulating. Asymmetrical balance appears dynamic and as animated as an elm tree. In nature, symmetry is rare, while asymmetric balance is common.

There are many wind-swept trees, as well as bushes and vines overhanging a cliff that are stable even when inclined far from the vertical. Flower stalks that receive more light on one side than on the other may incline similarly. Because such growing trees, bushes, vines and flower stalks are fastened to the earth by their roots, they are stable, though they are not vertically erect.

Rhythm: A work of art in which the correlation of its parts produces a well-ordered, coherent design is said to possess rhythm. The succession of movements in the classic dances of Greece and the Orient, the succession of accented sounds of music and in poetry, are characterized by rhythm. Such art forms give the mind more pleasure than would be experienced from a succession of unordered motions and accents. The ordered relations of lines, forms, spaces, colors and tones in a design give us a similar satisfaction. Thus, there are rhythms that affect the eye, as well as those that affect the ear. In music and in poetry, rhythm is a matter of timing, whereas in the visual arts, it is a matter of space, color and value.

There is a so-called measure-rhythm, or rhythm of gradation, produced by gradual increase or decrease in the size of units in a flower arrangement; a shape-rhythm produced by repetitions of conspicuous lines of areas; a rhythm of radiation produced by the flow of lines from a point or from a line. There is also a value-rhythm, produced by repetitions or variations of light and shade, and there is a color-rhythm produced by repetitions or variations of color.

Harmonies: The unity of diverse elements is called harmony. Trees, branches and flowers are often used for decoration because of their diverse lines, forms, colors and tones. Often they exhibit rhythm and harmony to high degree. There is a shape-harmony that results from the use of shapes having lines that are similar. A group of anthuriums and roses would lack shape-harmony, as much as would a fox terrier with a tail shaped like that of a squirrel.

A group of elements of similar color tones is said to possess tone-harmony. With a group of flowers of different colors but of the same species, it is possible to produce a better tone-harmony than with flowers of different species. Out of a group of several flowers of different species or textures, it is difficult to construct a flower arrangement that will have good tone-harmony.

There should be harmony of structure in the elements of a design. Stiff vertical flower stems are not usually in accord with trailing vines.

A flower arrangement should be in harmony with its purpose. If intended to exert a calming effect on the mind of a person who is ill, flowers of delicate forms and colors should be used, and all aggressive color combinations should be avoided. All of the living elements of a flower arrangement should be those that naturally grow in the same environment and during the same season of the year. Highly-developed greenhouse flowers seldom harmonize with wild flowers from the woodlands.

A flower arrangement should be in accord with its container and its situation. A design consisting of short, delicately colored and daintily-shaped flowers in a low container of silver, glass or porcelain is appropriate for a dinner table decoration. A design consisting of a woody branch and tall flower stalks mounted in a tall, massive bronze container is appropriate for a position on the floor or heavy hall table. If these two designs were interchanged in position they would not harmonize with their surroundings.

Unity: The proper coordination of every element in a design, one to another, is called unity. Lines, areas and colors must be so related by their positions, shapes, hues and connections that the group will appear as a connecting whole. In order that a flower arrangement may possess artistic unity, the flowers must not differ too much in size, form, texture and natural

Figure 25.

All components of the design are beautifully related through compatibility of line, form, color and texture.

habitat. The curves of all branches, stems and the container must be in accord. A sunflower would not go well with a pansy, a hydrangea with a gardenia, a delicate rose with a coarse zinnia, a pond-lily with a carnation, or a calla lily with a violet.

Expression Through Form: Usually designs are based upon some simple geometric figure, such as the circle (Raphael's *Madonna della Sedia*), the triangle (Raphael's *Sistine Madonna*), or the letter "L" (as seen in many landscapes).

The triangle is a common shape in nature, observable in the outlines of mountains, rocks, trees and plants. The scalene triangle, with its three unequal sides and angles, is especially esteemed as a basic of design because this triangle is subject to the greatest variation in shape. It is possessed of both unity and diversity, those essential characteristics of good design. When lying on its long side, the figure has the appearance of repose. When standing erect on its acute angle, it gives the impression of stateliness and power. When standing in an inclined position, it expresses dynamic force. The scalene triangle challenges the resourceful designer because of the variety of problems it presents in making it appear to have the proper degree of stability in its many possible attitudes.

Graceful curves and soft harmonies of color and form are conducive to contemplation, peace and contentment. Rugged shapes and dissonant empty spaces are expressive of intense emotion. The rhythms of spaces, line, form, color and tone furnish as great a range of expression as does intonation in speech or in music. The impression made by a group of flowers depends not only upon the plant material and the manner in which it is arranged in the container, but also upon the emotion felt by the composer and the sensitivity of the viewer. A Chinese art student is admonished, "The idea should be clear in the mind before the brush touches the inkstone."

In order that an artist working in any medium may be able either to express thoughts through his art, or to evoke thoughts and emotions in the beholder of his work, he must have clearly defined thoughts and intense emotion. He cannot either express or evoke a thought he does not intensely feel. The true floral artist then feels, sees and expresses his or her emotions in the work created.

Figure 26.

Gracefully flowing circles of bent rattan and looped New Zealand flax leaves emphasize the feeling of meditation and contemplation suggested by the carved wooden Madonna. The use of two containers, with one recessed, increases the impression of depth.

Choosing a Container

Often the most important form within any floral design is the container. The selection of this dominant form will either add deciding factors to the overall finished product, or be so completely disassociated with motivated intent that the entire design will fall short of seeming to be a finished product. Careful consideration must be given in choosing a container for any floral design. In most cases, the container should be the starting, deciding factor in the creation of any design. In other words, start with the container, then choose plant materials that will go well with the container and that will work well in the container. In short, this means that there should be a happy marriage between the container and all components chosen for placement in the container. There are certain qualities any container must possess. These qualities can be quickly decided by asking yourself a few simple questions.

- Is the container heavy enough (actually and visually) to hold the desired materials?
- Is the container conducive to the period or style of the planned design?
- Is the color appropriate for the other chosen components?
- Is the texture pleasing with the selected components?
- Is the container in scale with the other components?
- Is the container of proper proportion for use in the space in which the design is to be placed?
- Is the container functional? Does it allow the freedom needed to create the design pattern you have selected?
- Is there adequate space for water to keep the design fresh?
- Will the container hold the proper mechanics?
- Are there distinctive qualities in the container's color, form and texture?

After it has been decided that the chosen container fills the requirements, then go on with selecting the proper plant materials to create the design. There are many things one may use as a container. The creative person will often select something others may not have thought of as being usable as a container. The seeing eye can develop a sensitivity as to what will function as a container, and the most creative designs are those created by these designers. The following objects may be used as containers:

- Handmade ceramic pots designed for flowers.
- Traditional art forms considered as containers from different periods of history, namely: ewers, vases, pitchers, urns, bowls.
- Art forms, such as carved figures of people, animals, etc. Often a cup needlepoint holder is placed behind these figures to secure plant materials and hold water.
- Unusual pieces of weathered wood such as a palm spathe may be used to hold a cup needlepoint holder.
- Creative forms that hold water, chosen by the artist.
- Sea shells or other objects, such as concave rocks, that allow a needlepoint holder and water to be added.

Figure 27.

The interesting pottery container is eminently suited for use with the bold forms of the skeletonized Saguarro cactus, hosta leaves and dried banksia flowers.

Traditional and Creative Containers

One must be careful in selecting a container if a certain type of Traditional Design is to be created. Consideration should be given to historical records as to what type containers were used for certain period designs It is most important that the container be proper and in keeping with the style of design one creates. The choice of a container and of all plant materials will decidedly determine the type of period design you create. Certain type containers were used in each specific period, and it is important that containers and other components relate accurately to the period chosen for re-creation.

In choosing creative containers, the container must be of good color, form and texture to give distinctive qualities to the design's concept. While good reproductions of period containers are often used with great success, the creative design allows more freedom in the choice of containers. A strong geometric form may be the desired shape. Often a decorative design (one created to decorate one's home, church or club) may demand a European or Oriental flavor, because of surrounding decor. If this is the case, then choose a container that is in harmony with its setting.

One should start slowly in collecting a good supply of containers. A few well-chosen, functional containers of good quality will be of greater value to a designer than a larger collection of cheap containers that don't quite come up to requirements of today's designs. Select only those that will fill these requirements. Many of us work in only one style, so our choice in selection should be quite easy. If a container meets requirements with respect to color, form, texture and total design, then you will find a way to use it. In having fun with arranging, the right container can always be a joy.

Figure 28.

An antique copper lustre urn holds a decorative design of massed flowers having warm colors.

Creative and Abstract Design Containers

In Creative and Abstract designs, the container's construction usually must be a form having more than one opening at or near the top. In designs of this type, we must distribute the materials used so as to create more than one area of interest within the design. In doing this, it is impossible to place materials in these positions when there is only one opening at the top of the container. Several functional openings must be found to allow freedom in placing the plant materials. These openings should either be large enough to place needle holders in the container, or small enough to hold stems by wedging them in place. Considerations should be made during the construction or selection of the pot, as these openings must be placed at the proper angle to allow directional placement of materials in order to achieve balance in the final construction of the design.

The theory in using a container in these creative abstract designs is that we use the container as a forceful form within the total pattern of the design. Materials are not only brought from the top of the container, but are anchored lower in the container in openings, circle the container, or rise from behind the container. In some rare cases, materials may be placed so as to achieve all these concepts. Materials may often touch the table or base and only contact the container for balance; thus the container becomes the needed balance factor.

Whenever possible, the color of the container should be repeated in materials chosen to be placed in the container. If this is impossible, the background color should be one that will keep the container from seeming out of place; we can always control the design by selecting the proper background. Be very careful in the selection of a container. If the container seems overpowering, then this will affect design principles, namely rhythm; if the container is forceful, the eye will never leave this force, causing lack of movement in the design. If the container size is too large, it may not allow you to choose larger materials to complete a design that will fit the allotted space. Remember that balance includes the total design; the heavy container will create visual weight in the lower frame of reference, which will disturb the total balance.

One's needs in a design concept can often be met with just the right container: for instance, color can be quietly fused in a harmonious selection of all components by using the right container. However, you may select a container to create sharp contrast in the design. When this is done, careful consideration is again important.

Any selected container must have enough actual weight to mechanically hold the chosen plant materials. Often ceramic containers are not heavy enough to achieve proper balance when plant materials are added. If this is true, then add sand or small pebbles to the bottom of the container until you have achieved stability and balance in the design. A good ceramic container should be "wheel thrown," and the walls should be at least 1/4" thick. This will give enough strength in the construction to prevent breakage if pressure is applied by the designer when anchoring heavy plant materials in the design.

In theory, then, a creative abstract designer may use anything as a container as long as it does not have strong conventional or traditional characteristics. If a container has these characteristics, it will appear out of character, for it will not relate well to the other components in the design.

Figure 29.

The design seems to grow out of the highly creative container. Another interesting feature is the selection of small rattan forms, used as accessories in the design.

Good Taste Makes The Difference

Some people like clam chowder with milk, but no tomatoes; others like it better with tomatoes, but no milk. Some appreciate and enjoy fine wines; others cannot taste or smell the difference between a fine vintage wine and a wine produced in bulk. There are those who like the subjective, highly emotional, expressionist flower arrangements. Others consider this type of creative design a kind of repulsive, psychopathological catharsis. Some think that the polytonal compositions of Bela Bartok and Darius Milhaud are a peculiarly unpleasant and complicated kind of noise, while others enjoy hearing them. Few subjects can involve so many other areas as do flower arrangements; food, drink, furniture, manners, aesthetics can all be involved. Floral designs can be controversial and heatedly argued with regard to questions of taste.

Our aesthetic judgment is constantly being challenged by problems of choice similar to those presented in any given taste test. Which dress? Which chair? Which tie? Which design? We make these or similar decisions of taste every day, and we must often justify our decisions. Nor is it always possible to sidestep the situation as adroitly as did Abraham Lincoln who, when cornered and forced to express his judgment of some very controversial material, said, "For the sort of person who likes this sort of thing, this is just the sort of thing that those sorts of people would like very much." But in some instances we might justly defend our choice by quoting the old proverb, "There is no disputing taste." For example, our preferring Notre

Dame de Paris to either the Parthenon or the Taj Mahal may not, perhaps, be disputed. Each is superlative in its class, and our choice may be based on purely personal preference rather than aesthetic judgment. But a preference for Bach versus boogie-woogie, or Cézanne versus calendar art should admit to more valid dispute. If it does not, then aesthetic standards are meaningless.

For centuries artists and philosophers have been arguing over aesthetic standards. These disputes have sometimes been confused and futile because aesthetic judgment or taste is often subconsciously influenced by many biasing or nonaesthetic factors. Racial, religious, moral, social, political and nationalistic prejudices, personal predilection for the old and familiar or the new and novel, and fashion or gregarious herd instinct, are molded by these factors. Many persons may affect the protective pose of fashionable taste because they are afraid to stand alone, or do not trust their aesthetic judgment. Even such a courageous and honest man as George Bernard Shaw said, "Even if I did not like Mozart, I should pretend to; for a taste for his music is a mark of caste among musicians, and should be worn, like a tall hat, by an amateur who wishes to pass for a true Brahmin."

Fashion, that blind, unreasoning, and undiscriminating instinct, is exploited by hucksters of everything from whiskey to movies to political and medical nostrums. These merchants of mediocrity profitably spend millions of advertising dollars each year to assure us that millions of our gullible fellow-sheep eat, drink, smoke, read, wear or use this product, and that, therefore, it must be good. For many people this appeal to fashion seems to carry as much weight as the Ten Commandments or the Constitution. Having the courage to resist mob propaganda and stand up for one's aesthetic convictions should not be confused with stubborn, intolerant smugness.

In addition to the personal prejudices and nonaesthetic biases previously mentioned, disputes about taste are often confused by disagreements on the following questions. What exactly does aesthetic taste mean? According to Webster, one of the accepted authorities on definitions, aesthetic taste is the "power of discerning and appreciating beauty, order, proportion, etc., in the fine arts and belles-lettres; critical judgment, discernment of what is pleasing, refined, or good usage; as a man of taste." Taste, therefore, means good taste, or the faculty of aesthetic appreciation and discernment possessed by both the observer and the creator of a fine design. Bad taste means a lack of aesthetic judgement or an absence of this critical faculty.

Taste may also mean an inseparable property, quality, attribute or aspect of the design, because the design inevitably exhibits or expresses the taste or lack of taste of the designer. This is what is meant when it is said that a design is in good (or in bad) taste. It would therefore, be contradictory to say, "It is a good design, but in bad taste," or "It is a bad design, but in good taste," because good design is good taste, and bad design is bad taste.

Is taste purely personal? "No," says W. C. Brownell in *Standards*. "Taste is essentially a matter of tradition. No one originates his own."

Is good taste an inherited ability, faculty or talent? "No," says Augustine Birrell, "You may as well expect to be born with a high silk hat on your head as with good taste." In *Patience*, W. S. Gilbert says, "You can't get high aesthetic tastes, like trousers, ready-made." William Wordsworth agrees, and thinks, "An accurate taste in poetry, as in all other arts, is an acquired talent, which can only be produced by severe thought and a long-continued intercourse with the best models of composition." But others believe that taste may be improved by education, practice and experience. Perhaps this question may eventually be decided by the psychologists.

Can good taste be taught by rules? Although principles of aesthetic order can be taught, no intelligent person believes that good taste or genius can be acquired by learning a set of "rules." How can you tell good taste from bad taste? There is, of course, no easy, infallible way for you to decide. For you, a thing is in good taste if you honestly consider that it can be justly characterized as integrated, well-proportioned, beautiful, interesting, original, creative, fine, sincere appropriate, clean, logical, direct and efficient. For you, a thing is in bad taste if you sincerely feel that it can be fairly described as chaotic, confused, illogical, badly proportioned, ugly, inappropriate, shoddy, cheap, common, ordinary, trite, insincere, affected, showy, gaudy, garish, vulgar, cute, etc.

There are, of course, many degrees or levels of taste, ranging from the abysmally bad, to mediocre, to superlatively good. Although the arbiters of taste might disagree with your aesthetic judgment and classifications, these represent your honest, if personal, aesthetic yardstick that you can develop and refine, if you will. Our standards of taste are constantly changing, as we grow. As we develop finer discrimination, keener perception, maturer appreciation, we may discover that our old aesthetic yardsticks, tags and labels have become ludicrously inadequate and must be revised or discarded.

Who are the arbiters of taste? They may be critics or creators, amateurs or professionals, spectators or performers. They may be on all economic levels. They may be collectors of expensive, autographed copies of limited editions, or they may be buyers of cheap reprints. At the opera, they may relax in their private boxes, or they may stand in the gallery. They may be articulate or inarticulate. They may be professors in obscure colleges, their ideas unknown beyond the campus. And they may be quiet, anonymous but discerning people whose approval or disapproval is perhaps expressed only by the books, tickets, music records, or art they buy or do not buy. In our field, they may be the Master Judge, the Student Judge, the advanced arranger or the novice arranger who is just beginning. They may be of different races, religions or political beliefs.

But whatever else they may be, they are a brotherhood that has these characteristics in common: deep interest in an appreciation of a particular art form; a conviction that it is an important part of living; mature, unbiased judgment based on knowledge of, and wide experience with, the best works in their field; and severe, uncompromising standards of performance. These are the jury of the cognoscente, the connoisseurs who establish our aesthetic criteria. These are the brotherhood of the elite, the arbiters of taste and the custodians of our cultural heritage. Perhaps these few words will help you in becoming a member of this essential brotherhood in floral artistry.

To create any good flower arrangement, it is not enough to know the relationships of color and form and to apply the laws that govern them; the designer must also strive to free him or herself from the servitude inherent in such a task. Any arranger of healthy sensitivity and sufficient intelligence can provide us with well-made designs; but only he/she who was directed by taste can awaken beauty. We reject the notions of good taste and bad taste, which correspond with nothing positive: a faculty is neither good or bad, it is simply more or less developed.

We attribute a rudimentary taste to the native who is delighted by glass beads or a sea shell, but we might with infinitely greater justice consider as a savage the so-called civilized man who, for example, can appreciate nothing but Italian paintings or Louis XV furniture. Taste is valued according to the number of qualities it allows us to perceive; yet when the number exceeds a certain figure, it diminishes in intensity and evaporates into eclecticism. Taste is innate; but like sensitivity, which enhances it, it is tributary to the will. Many deny this. What is more obvious, however, than the influence of the will on our senses? It is so apparent that as soon as we could wish it, we could isolate the high-pitched note of an oboe among the metallic thunders of an orchestra. Similarly, we can succeed in savoring a certain quality whose existence is affirmed by reason alone.

Is the influence of the will upon taste intrinsically good or evil? The will can only develop taste along a plane parallel to that of the consciousness.

The secret to good taste in any design lies within the realm of selectivity and restraint. One must not choose materials at random, but rather should select and reject with care, where one seems to belong, another will be totally out of character. Designers are often forced to use what is at hand. In other words, it is not often that one always has just the right thing when a design is being developed.

In developing total form of any design, many materials may be tried before there becomes a fusion of unity within the combined materials. A unity of forms must exist. It is within the total form (the completed design) that one seeks ultimate taste and restraint. There must be the right textural, color, line and form contrasts within the design form to express good taste. A happy marriage of all the elements, guided by the principles of design, will result in a design of restraint. Restraint comes naturally to any design that has limited the numbers and kinds of materials selected to create its total form.

Expression

Expression is the most difficult aspect of creating a design, especially in creative concepts. Most people become totally literal in trying to express a class title and, in so doing, neglect the basic principles that govern all designs. There doesn't seem to be a ready answer to the problem. All flower shows have a theme, and in classes for design, the theme is carried out with class titles. Let's face it, it is much easier to create just a Creative Design than to create a design with a title. For instance, a class titled "Sunset," asking for a creative design staged against a background, becomes both an emotional and mechanical problem. The title is limited to some extent because the title itself suggests certain things that are governed by literal presentation.

When a design becomes too literal, it loses spontaneity, which is a hallmark of true creative concept. The creative artist who strives to avoid literal interpretation totally can become "so far out" with his work that the average judge cannot comprehend what is presented, and the award may be placed on a design of lesser quality. When this is done, the artist does not understand and his spirit is repressed.

Now, a short and clear statement about restraint: We can best define restraint by saying it is "less of more." Try not to use more than two or three types of plant material in any design. Using more often creates a problem in organization, as well as diffusing the visual impact that is needed to make a good design become more outstanding and creative. It might be said that a story told in a few important words is more lasting in our memory span than a rambling, lengthy story. Therefore, a good expressive design has both good taste and restraint in its visual impact.

Figure 30.

Two carved, painted parrots, used with small ears of dried corn and miniature orchids, combine into a uniquely creative design. The many openings of the pottery container lend themselves to varied placement of the materials.

CHAPTER FOUR

The Elements and Principles of Design

THE PLASTIC ELEMENTS

Poets and novelists use words—nouns, pronouns, verbs, adjectives and adverbs—when they verbally express their ideas. Composers use varied tonal sounds to express musical ideals; and artists, whether painters, architects, industrial designers or flower arrangers, use the plastic elements—FORM, LINE, SPACE, TEXTURE and COLOR—when they express their plastic or graphic ideas.

The plastic elements are the ingredients or constituents of the plastic arts. A human arm, for example, is cylindrical in *form*, light red-orange in *color*, and soft and smooth in *texture*. Its edges can be interpreted as *lines* and it exists in *space*. Artists pay attention to these elements, not as separate or discrete aspects but as related components of what they see, touch or know.

Forms, lines, spaces, textures and colors are perceived in relationship to their surroundings, and those surroundings are of the greatest importance in the total effect. Imagine the pyramids of Egypt transformed from the sands of the desert to a valley in the Rocky Mountains. They would still be large, pyramidal and impressive, but in comparison with the towering peaks of the Rockies, the Pyramids would seem smaller and less significant than in their own environment.

Form

An understanding of form is essential to the appreciation of design, since forms, properly organized and basically related, are the first things considered in planning any floral arrangement.

Form is the sculptured mold, the outward appearance of anything three-dimensional. Shape applies to the two-dimensional. The shape of a leaf has length and width, the form of an orange has length, depth and width. A flower painted on a canvas has shape, but a flower growing in your garden has form.

Every floral arrangement is a physical structure. It must have the strength to stand. The elements of texture and color should enhance the various forms that go into making up the whole, relieving them of monotony and bareness, but the strength of the design must be built from within. A child playing with blocks selects certain forms to provide a foundation for his or her construction. The child quickly learns to use large blocks as a base to support smaller blocks in the building.

A good phrase to remember is Thomason's "form follows function," for design is based on simple logic, and function is the efficient use of something that is particularly well adapted to a specific purpose. It is a plan to follow when making anything exactly right for its special use. The human body is a good example of true functionalism. The hand, for instance, can do almost anything the mind suggests. The four fingers and thumb make up a highly efficient tool. The loss of even one finger impairs the hand's effectiveness; the addition of another would make it clumsy. So it is with each part of the body. Function is the prime requisite. Beauty is a secondary consideration. When an engineer designs a bridge, his first concern must be whether it will bear the loads to which it will be subjected. Will this bridge meet the demands made of it? The beauty of the finished structure will stem from true functionalism.

In the selection of plant materials, it is essential to keep in mind the functions of various forms, which are considered under three broad classifications: ROUNDED FORMS, TRANSITIONAL FORMS and ELONGATED FORMS.

Rounded Forms: These forms are commanding and confine the eye to a concentric circle. They convey a feeling of isolation. They do not blend easily into the background and hold themselves aloof from adjacent materials. Rounded forms usually appear to have weight and bulk. They are used where compelling strength and eye appeal are needed.

Nature is very seldom repetitious. While general characteristics are found in all rounded forms, each has its own distinguishing aspect, its own identity. Therefore, each must be considered for its own unique contribution. An orange is a rounded form, both solid and heavy, and its outline is regular. An iris is a rounded form, but it is not a solid, nor does it have visual weight. It is delicate and space is an important part of its design. The more ruffled and uneven its petals, the more eye appeal it will have. The fragile iris is incompatible with structurally heavy components.

Most rounded forms have a decided magnetic pull. This is particularly true of deep-throated flowers, such as the lily. Others, like the agapanthus, have sunbursts of small, unimportant blooms that radiate outward and so lessen that tensional pull. When you look at any floral design, your eye seeks a path to travel. A good design should have an area of interest so magnetic that you are compelled to stop and consider it. To supply this area of accelerated interest is the prime function of the rounded form. But the rest of the composition must not be forced into the background. If the focal area is too powerful, it is difficult to see less vibrant parts of the design and the whole arrangement becomes static. Rounded forms, such as marigolds, full-blown roses, zinnias and peonies, command such attention that we must be led away from them by gradual transition.

Elongated Forms: These forms have a line-like quality. They usually become more and more slender until they seem to be part of the surrounding space. This slender material, which flows with such ease into nothingness, gives charm and character to the silhouette of the design, and as it tapers off in size and importance, the eye is lured back into the area of dominant interest. This is the function of all elongated material, to create lines that travel into space. Branches and scotch broom are fine examples of line-like materials. Flowers such as larkspur, snapdragon and stock, are composed of small, rounded florets so closely grouped on the stem as to give them the directional force of an elongated form.

Transitional Forms: These forms, found in profusion in plant materials, act as peace-makers. They reconcile and unify contrasting materials. Their function is to establish a relationship between the rounded forms and the elongated forms that make up the silhouette of any design. They lead away from the area of interest by gradual transition, repeating some qualities of consistent likeness, while introducing others for a calculated change. Some examples of transitional forms are lilac, slender tulips, roses in the bud stage, clusters of berries, etc.

The form of a flower may depend upon its stage of development. A fully opened rose is a rounded form, but a tight bud on a long stem is an elongated form. The outline of plant material will suggest its use in a design. Turn it and see how its outline changes, then select the angle best suited for your purpose. Forms that are strong and bold must be placed where strength and interest are needed. Eye appeal and size diminish as lines extend upward. Each form is turned in a way to fill a given space. When a designer lacks the technique to fit these forms together, unoccupied spaces become holes in the design. A hole can be a misplaced void. If a hole develops in the area of accelerated interest, it is possible to fill it with materials that do not assert themselves, such as leaves. But this is only a trick and does not minimize the importance of correct placement.

Figure 31.

The magnificent piece of curly monkey puzzle vine, the bold red forms of heliconia blossoms and the heavy round form of the container all combine into one cohesive design, which emphasizes the dominance of FORM.

The form of an entire arrangement must be considered, as well as the forms of the individual plant materials. Here the designer is not limited to three broad classifications. There are many geometric shapes whose balance and proportion have stood the test of time. The crescent, the Hogarth curve, the semicircle and the spiral are all derived from the roundness of the globe. The triangle, vertical and horizontal designs are from the rectangle. You may choose one of these forms to guide you, but to make a mechanical reproduction would rob your materials of their naturalness and vitality.

Depth is another aspect of form to be considered. There must be a developed foreground, middleground and background in every flower arrangement, even if it is to be viewed from only one side. It is possible to contour and give a third dimension to a design by letting a few flowers or leaves overlap others. The eye of the observer can be guided to the flowers in the background by using carefully graded color values, such as light to dark. This can be better understood with a deeper study of color use.

The container plays an important part in the form of an arrangement and must be chosen with that in mind. It also has length, width and depth, though it may be self-effacing and blend so easily into the picture that the flowers seem to grow out of it. On the other hand, there are containers like those used in Creative Designs, which are such interesting forms in themselves that they set the style of the entire design.

Biomorphic forms are abundant in nature. Pears and squash, eggs, our own ears, eyes and hearts are but a few examples. They are the forms connected with life and growth. They have been literally copied, noticeably modified or completely abstracted.

Line

Lines and shapes can express ideas even when abstracted. When we are tired and lie down to sleep, we assume a horizontal position. Invariably the things that mean repose to us are horizontal objects, such as large calm bodies of water or low rolling hills and meadows. When we are up and about, we move in a vertical position, and when vertical lines are seen in pictures with horizontal lines, the vertical lines look more awake and strong. When we run or are otherwise active, our bodies assume a diagonal position, head thrust forward, balance somewhat precarious, elbows and knees forming angles. It seems then that the expressiveness of lines (and forms too) has its basis in human experience. Certainly we know that an artist may make a building, a statue or a piece of furniture look restful or imposing or excited and moving.

Figure 32. (Opposite)
Strongly vertical lines are created by the dried yucca stems, with another stem placed on the diagonal. The giant strelitzia blooms repeat the same lines, with the curved lines of the container providing pleasing contrast.

Line, however, is not always used to express deep human emotion and experience. Often it is used to merely represent objects: a line drawing of a building; lines drawn on maps to represent rivers, roads or contours; or lines drawn on paper all represent words. Such use of line is primarily utilitarian, a convenient way of communicating our ideas to another person. Whatever the emphasis, expression of human emotion or representation of factual materials, line is an important plastic element at the disposal of the artist.

Qualities of line:

- Line results from a point that has been set in motion, creating movement, which may be curved, angular, etc.
- Line travels vertically, horizontally, diagonally or in a circular direction
- Line possesses size, form, weight, color and texture
- Line divides space, gives outline to form and travels at various rates of speed

Function of line:

- To create movement within the design
- To express a theme
- To represent symbolism
- To provide the structure or foundation of design

Concept of line includes:

- Communication
- Quality
- Versatility
- Dimension
- Direction
- Distance
- Boundary
- Space
- Planes
- Defines form by outline
- Structure
- Temperature (cold, horizontal)
- Ritual
- Calligraphy
- Visual tension (point to point)
- Line segment

Space

When Mozart was asked what was the most beautiful music, he said, "No music." He meant, of course, the moments of pause and rest, of total silence. In Mozart's own scores, there are moments of no music, a hundredfold more eloquent than the music that surrounds them. We are also familiar with the dramatic pauses used by actors on the stage or screen and by speakers on the platform to emphasize a point or a mood. Often one word has more effect than a thousand could.

Space is the corresponding element in the plastic arts. It has been said that the reality of architecture resides in the space rather than in the mass. Certainly it is the space we use, and for spiritual or utilitarian reasons, contemporary architects are focusing their attention on spatial organization. Walls, floors and ceilings are certainly necessary and important, but their most significant meaning is derived from the space they make usable and satisfying. Since the dawn of history, man has sought space sufficiently enclosed to protect him, yet open enough for his body and soul. Natural caves were readymade solutions for primitive man; then came the massive Egyptian structures in which thick walls provided security, but minimized openness. Later the Greeks, Romans and Gothic builders succeeded in making buildings with more and more flexible space. Present-day architecture accelerates these trends by using new materials and methods heretofore unavailable, therefore encouraging this strong desire for spaciousness. Gardens, too, are compositions in space. Trees, shrubs, fences and buildings are vertical divisions. Lawns or pavements serve as floors, and sky, trees, or trellises act as ceilings. Beyond houses and gardens are communities, which are also organizations of space.

We turn from these gigantic examples of space organization to the graphic arts, which deal with symbolic rather than actual space, specifically design with flowers. Space should never be thought of as leftover area, which happened not to be filled with parts of the arrangement, nor as a void of nothingness. Space must be considered and used for what it is: an absolute essential of the life and expressiveness of every design. There cannot be an arrangement without space. On the other hand, there cannot be a concept of space without objects to delineate it. In experiencing a design, sometimes the space will take on dominant importance, at other times the objects. Between these two optical and emotional pulls, the movement and form of the design is created.

Dimensions are a humanly created method for measuring and evaluating space. Space has only those dimensions that we impose on it or project into it. We must do this in order to find our relationship to space and to have an understandable and manageable area in which to work. The limiting, man-made boundaries give a frame of reference against which and in which we are able to orient ourselves. A boundary represents a field of space in which to place and relate the elements of a design. The designer may work on a two-dimensional plane of space, or in a three-dimensional volume of space. The artist who is painting a picture, working in two dimensions, uses the boundaries of this chosen plane as a fixed measurement. This outer edge is called a *frame of reference*; the inner area, or two-dimensional plane, is called the *picture plane*. An artist creates an illusion of three-dimensional space by the placement of light and shadows, or light and dark values of color to cause shapes to appear to advance beyond or recede into the picture plane.

Three-dimensional space is actual space in which we can physically move. Since we do not have a constant frame of reference, we ourselves become the measure of space and equilibrium. We assume the role of horizontal and vertical axis. Visually we project this axial measurement from ourselves to some object that we consider to be in equilibrium: a wall, a window, tabletop or tree. This becomes our reference area. An artist, who works in three-dimensional media, designs with his eye not on the shallow frontal plane, but on the back spatial boundary. The three-dimensional space in which the flower arranger works is a shallow, volumetric space. The artist dealing with a two-dimensional medium works in deep illusionary space. In sculpture or in flower arrangement, the eye moves around, over and into the design.

It is very important that arrangers realize the characteristics and qualities of volumetric space, and create within its limitations. The arrangement that is related only to a two-dimensional frontal frame of reference can be nothing but a flat facade. It is a great help when beginning a design, and throughout its creation, to try to see and feel the space/object relationship of the place where the design is to be displayed. This space is the field of force that suggests the scale, rhythm, interest and shape of the composition. It will also be helpful to "work around" a composition. The designer will be taking advantage of the qualities that three-dimensional spaces offer.

Suggestions for helping to develop a sense of space:

- Think of space as real material, not a void.

- Visualize the larger space where the design will ultimately be placed ("think around" the arrangement).

- Avoid working in a crowded or cluttered area.

- Turn the arrangement often as you proceed.

- As each piece of material is added, check its relationship not only to the other materials, but to the space created around it. Make sure that this space is interesting and well balanced.

Figure 33. *(Opposite)*
The monkey puzzle vine and the pottery container both contain interesting enclosed spaces within them, enhancing the design.

Figure 34.

Another design illustrating the dynamic quality of space. Here, unoccupied spaces
are as important as the occupied spaces to the overall impact of the design.

Color

In one of Dicken's books there is a conversation between two stable boys in which one tries to get the other to visualize a world without color: grass that is not green and sky that is not blue. The other boy is not bright enough to handle such an idea and wonders vaguely about his companion's sanity. It is difficult to imagine a colorless world. We cannot blame the second boy for refusing to enter a discussion with his friend. We also would think the subject not worth discussing. Nature without color is unthinkable.

In recent years, the attitude of people toward color has changed as decorators have learned its power. In one factory, female workers complained of the cold although the temperature was 72 degrees. The blue-green walls were repainted coral and the complaints ceased. In another, men who lifted black boxes complained of strained backs. When the same boxes were painted a pale green, they said the new "light-weight" boxes made a real difference.

There are other facets of color: flies tend to avoid blue, and night flying insects keep away from orange light bulbs. Barnacles, pests of the shipping industry, avoid ship hulls in light colors, seeking those that are dark. Clearly, color is a powerful force.

Without light, there is no color, because color *is* light. Physicists tell us that white (or apparently colorless) light, such as that furnished by the sun at midday, contains all the colors of the spectrum. These colors are so balanced and blended that the effect is white. When this light strikes an object, certain colors are absorbed, others are reflected. We recognize three distinct color qualities, which are:

1. *Hue*, which refers to the spectrum sensation of redness, greenness, etc.

2. *Value*, which refers to the range from dark to light.

3. *Intensity*, which refers to the brightness or dullness of the hue.

As with shape, color qualities change in relation to their relative positions and also in relation to our distance from them. Value can be changed by relationship. Darks appear darker and lights appear lighter when they are placed next to each other. A flower of light value may look very light when placed next to a dark leaf, but quite dark when placed next to another flower or leaf of a value lighter than itself. When it is desirable to cause a flower to appear more dominant, naturally the fullest possible intensity of the color should be utilized, but with background colors, choose the greatest possible contrast. If the flower is small, it should be of the highest intensity. This is called "the law of areas." There are other useful guides to the use of color.

Equality of hue, value and intensity is not as satisfying as intentional diversity, because equality gives little emphasis or contrast. Equality of sizes in area of color is as unsatisfying as equality of hue, value or intensity. Intensity can be changed by relationship. We may see a hue simply as yellow, until another yellow is placed near to it. Then we may see the first yellow as greenish or reddish, depending on the quality and quantity of the second yellow.

Color Mixtures: Countless color sensations can be derived by combining the three color qualities. The mixture may be made directly with light, as when a spotlight is used on the stage, or by the blending of pigments. The light method is called *additive*. The blending of pigments is the *subtractive* method. The difference is the way in which the color qualities are achieved.

We know that white is made up of all the hues in light. When yellow, blue, red and green are mixed or added together the result is white. When yellow, blue, red and green pigments are mixed the result is black. This is because pigments selectively absorb or subtract hues from light. When all hues are absorbed we see black. When none is subtracted, we see white. When a blue or red or any other hue is seen, it is because the pigment has subtracted all others and reflected only one.

By either method, hue, value and intensity can be changed. The *primary* hues of light are yellow, blue and red. These are called primary because all other secondary hues can be made from them. When similar compatible hues are blended (yellow and red, red and blue, blue and green, and green and yellow), intermediate or analogous hues are created. *Analogous* colors are related neighboring hues. Dissimilar, antagonistic hues are called *complementary* colors. When complementary hues are mixed, the result is not a new hue, but a decrease in intensity. When the mixture is of certain proportions, all hue is lost and we see only gray. Colors of low intensity are often referred to as grayed colors.

Black and white are antagonistic, or complementary. The intermediate grays of their blending are values, the degree of lightness or darkness, or between the two poles of light and no light. Every blending, whether it be additive or subtractive, affects the hue, the intensity and the value of color, depending on the combinations and the amounts used.

Visual Mixtures: There is a third way by which colors are mixed, a blending that takes place in the eye. Scientists have determined that the eye sees color by means of three color nerves, which are sensitive to red, blue and yellow-green light. From blendings of these three sensations, we are able to experience all color. The selected color that enters the eye comes from either a pigment or a direct light stimulant. The eye must recreate this experience. In doing so, it experiences the color in relation to amount, saturation, and position.

If we are forced to look too long at one color, such as red, the nerve for that color becomes fatigued and automatically switches to the complementary green nerve, then we see an after-image of green. An equal strength of two complementary colors will cause the eye to twitch, to fluctuate between two, often with an after-image of gray or yellow. This is frequently experienced with arrangements of red roses or poinsettias. A green or yellow reverse image can be seen in the center of the flower. When the fluctuation is too great, this can be a very uncomfortable sensation.

Analogous colors, when placed in certain relationships, often visually mix with their complements. When reds or yellows are placed together, the eye may not see orange, but green in the yellow, or blue in the red, thus visually mixing a yellow-green or a red-purple. Many small points of color are mixed by the eye. This visual mixture in art is called *pointillism*. By this method, hue, value and intensity are modified. Value can be changed by interspersing dark and light points. Analogous hues can be created by making point groupings. Red and yellow zinnias, for example, can be so placed as to give a sensation of orange. Blue and purple flowers grouped together appear to be an intermediate hue. When points of complementary

Figure 35.
A very pleasing
design proves that
using only one color
can be interesting if
careful attention is
paid to contrast in
texture and form.

colors are so placed that they will visually mix, the intensity of colors is lowered. No set rule can be given for visual mixture. When we understand the general way mixtures are created and controlled, we can experiment and train our eyes to sensitivity. Of the three ways color can be modified—by additive, subtractive and visual mixtures—the arranger is concerned primarily with visual mixture. Additive mixture of direct light source should be considered by the arranger especially in the staging of exhibition work. Dramatic effects can be created by the use of colored spotlights. Pigmentation mixture does not overly concern the arranger, since this is done for the arranger by nature. In the province of flower arranging, it is mostly a matter of training the eye to see and select.

In Creative Designs, colors are utilized for their part in the total effect. The greatest emphasis in Creative Design is on form, which is often exaggerated. Primary lines are often far taller in contemporary designs. Color appeals directly to the emotions. The message made apparent by the design can be more readily understood if hues of high intensity are utilized. Great contrast in hues is compatible to modern ideas in decorating. Containers show earthy tones, and the use of symbolic hues is currently much in vogue.

Texture

You have seen how form, lines and spaces play their parts in giving character to art objects. You have seen, as our study progressed, how another element, texture, has tried to assert itself in various forms and objects. You will be aware of this instantly if you close your eyes and run your fingers over this page, then over some article of clothing you are wearing, then over the table in front of you. Now try sandpaper, fur and glass. The fingers report differences: smoothness, roughness, silkiness. Texture is the surface quality of an object. Differences in texture can be as striking as roundness or squareness, which are differences in form, while red and green are differences in color.

Of the five plastic elements, texture deals most directly with the sense of touch. Surfaces produce tactile sensations when we touch them; these are called *tactile values*. Tactile values are best appreciated when an object is actually felt with the hands. This was brought sharply to the attention of the managers of a store that deals in women's clothing. In a newly-remodeled department, coats and dresses were kept in sight, but out of reach, behind glass doors. The customers objected. They wanted to *feel* the clothes. So it was found necessary to again alter the department so that the customers could feel what they were looking at. Because we touch clothes all the time, we become highly conscious of their tactile values. When we buy a dress or suit, one of our first impulses is to feel the material, because the hand as much as the eye aids in making the decision.

Texture is equally as important in architecture and furniture. Along with the other plastic elements, it contributes significantly to the total effect. Painters, too, are aware of the expressiveness of texture. Painters of the 18th and early 19th centuries placed high premiums on porcelain-like smoothness. The smoother the surface and forms, the more painters like Cézanne, Van Gogh, Picasso and other innovators began the exploration of textural possibilities. Contemporary painters and sculptors are exploring further the possibilities of textural values in their efforts to vitalize wood and stone.

Texture can be real or simulated. In some objects there are actual three-dimensional variations in the surface; in others, they are but two-dimensional patterns suggested by color differences.

Different types of texture in plant material: The tissue structure of plant material determines the actual texture or feel, and the way the surface is formed determines the visual texture. The surface of plant material often cannot be altered by the floral artist as can the media of other artists. For example, a potter can create a rough or smooth surface on his or her clay, but a floral artist is concerned with selecting textures already present in the plant material, harmonizing and contrasting them. There is a wealth from which to choose, and the greater variety offered by plant material is one of its most valuable assets. There are remarkable differences between the surface qualities, both actual and visual, of, for example, camellias,

Figure 36.
Contrast in textures—from the very smooth and satiny calla lilies, to the slightly rough strelitzia leaves, to the rough antlers and pottery container—contribute greatly to the interest and dramatic appeal of this design.

carnations, artichokes, chestnuts, teasels, pine cones and dock. Some plant material shows more than one texture: the horse chestnut is a good example of many contrasting textures in one tree, with its rough bark, matte leaf, sticky bud, glossy chestnut in a prickly outer covering and silky flowers.

There are many descriptive words that can be applied to plant material, such as:

leathery . . . delicate . . . bristly . . . fluffy . . . furry . . . coarse
sticky . . . downy . . . corky . . . shiny . . . polished . . . thorny
scratchy . . . fuzzy . . . dull . . . prickly . . . glossy . . . crepey
tough . . . feathery . . . crinkly . . . silky . . . rough . . . velvety
hairy . . . fine . . . rubbery . . . hard . . . crisp . . . waxy
firm . . . woolly . . . smooth . . . satiny . . . woody

The effect of texture: The texture of an object can make a great difference in its power for drawing the human eye. A shiny texture has great eye-pull, as it reflects the light so strongly. This means that a shiny container will need a design of plant material that is large or bold in comparison to attract the eye away from the container. Colored glass containers very easily dominate a design by their light reflection, so that the eye finds it difficult to travel to the plant material. A shiny object of any kind is more dominant than a dull one and can easily affect the visual balance of a design unless placed correctly. A small amount of shiny texture balances a much larger duller surface.

Texture greatly influences color. A carnation of the same red as a shiny poppy may appear darker because of the light being broken up by the carnation's texture. Lighting, too, makes a considerable difference. In very poor lighting little textural difference can be seen. Half-light often gives a more interesting sense of texture as the shadows are deeper, and full-light is not as enhancing. Exciting effects can be obtained by varying lighting so that it is stronger from one angle. If the plant material is turned to different angles, it will catch different lighting and give more interest.

Light

Light enhances the visual aspect of the total form. Light influences balance, depth, silhouette, texture, color, shapes and forms of the flower arrangement. Light accentuates dimensional planes through interpenetration of volumetric space. Mood in nature is also determined by the kind of light that falls on objects: a lyric, tender quality is imparted by a diffused light that blends the edges and shadows, leaving nothing harsh. Strong light emphasizes the edges of all objects equally, lending a matter-of-fact quality. Strong light centered in one area, but surrounded by dark, mysterious shadows, might suggest a dramatic mood. Lighting from below can cast eerie patterns of light on the background—this helps to break up the spaces and makes the picture more visibly interesting.

The artist has always depended on light to reveal and emphasize the beauty of form. Artificial lights are placed in such a way that they light the forms that are to be emphasized, to create patterns of light and shadow on details or features, to portray and regulate the shapes of spaces or shadows, to emphasize or establish a mood.

PRINCIPLES OF DESIGN

The principles of art are closely related to laws of nature. We did not invent them; we only discovered and formulated them. SCALE, RHYTHM, CONTRAST, PROPORTION, BALANCE and DOMINANCE are all aspects of a universal design that we, as flower arrangers, are just beginning to comprehend. We know, however, that to achieve unity in any art form, the elements of that art must be brought under control by these principles. When we learn to apply these principles to the art of flower arranging, we gain confidence in our own judgment, and no longer need to work by a set of hard and fast rules. Every art form demands a dedicated apprenticeship. Not only must we learn to see with greater clarity and open our minds to fresh ideas, but also our hands must develop new skills. We can only learn by doing. All the written words of artists and the hours spent in attending lectures and demonstrations cannot teach us as quickly as one good three-hour workshop, where we take the tools and media into our hands and create a design.

Rhythm

Rhythm is a pattern of movement in time and space. The entire universe is sustained by this important principle. We see it in the seasonal changes through the year, and as day turns to night, it is done with rhythmic grace. We see it in the ebb and flow of tides; we know it in the beat of our hearts. We walk in rhythm, talk in rhythm, run in rhythm. Most of us live in rhythmic life patterns.

In a flower arrangement we seek to create visual rhythm that we can see at a glance. In order to do this, we must select materials that have the needed qualities to establish rhythm, and then place them in logical sequence to form a pattern of change in direction or in one or more other qualities. There should be enough interesting intervals and pauses, resembling the rests in music, in order to hold the attention of the observer at a specific point before moving on to the rest of the design.

While rhythm is movement, not all movement is rhythmic. Rhythm is a means of linking one part to another in accordance with a pattern of time and motion. Materials having commanding form, compelling color, interesting texture or impressive size are said to have tensional pull. Be careful when using these materials because their use can affect rhythm. Rhythm also employs repetition. Variety is used to relieve the monotony of repetition, but do not interrupt the established rhythm with senseless diversion. Always remember that a rhythm controlled by carefully established relationships, including materials with sufficient strength and force, will command and hold attention.

Webster defines rhythm as "flow, movement, procedure, etc.; characterized by basically regular recurrence of elements or features, as beat, or accent, in alternation with opposite or different elements or features." In art, it is an aesthetic relationship of part to part and of parts to the whole. In flower arrangement, it is the flow of materials or colors of materials that carry the eye easily through the design. It is usually attained by the use of gradation, repetition and line direction.

Gradation is a sequence in which the adjoining parts are similar or harmonious. It implies gradual change: in size, from small to large; in weight, from heavy to light; in texture, from smooth to rough; in color, from light to dark, bright to dull, value to value, hue to hue. A traditional concept of design was that solidity at the base of the design and thinness at the extremities created rhythm, leading the eye easily through the design.

Repetition is achieved by repeating a shape, hue, value, direction, etc. However, exact repetition is monotonous so it should be modified, such as the use of pink for repetition of red; a grouping of small round forms to repeat a large round form; or several small straight lines to repeat a strong, large, straight line. There should be a dynamic use of line direction to carry the eye in a definite direction.

Figure 37.

Repetition created by the two placements of strelitizia flowers and pieces of weathered wood enhance the circular rhythm of the design.

Figure 38.

Placement of red anthuriums and aspidistra leaf serve to reinforce the rhythmic flow of the monkey puzzle vine.

Qualities Of Rhythm:

Connected Rhythm: Where gradation in size, form, color or texture is placed close together, in a step-by-step fashion to create an easy flow of the eye, the change is gradual and proceeds with ease.

Disconnected Rhythm: Like forms, colors, sizes and textures are distributed in a design in different areas, to create eye movement from one of these areas to another. There is no easy flow, however, because these like-impacts are so strong that through a play of planes on planes, a rhythm is created. The materials between these, or the spaces, become of secondary importance, and the eye movement is so strong that rhythm becomes evident.

Types Of Rhythm:

Natural Rhythm: Different types of rhythm are found in many plant materials. However, we must often make the viewer aware of this rhythm by pruning away the excess leaves or side branches to expose its beauty. These leaves and branches stop the natural flow of rhythm often found in the main stem of many tree materials.

Implied Rhythm: Means to suggest rhythm without openly or exactly expressing it. This can be done successfully by placing materials in areas in such a way that the designer's imagination is left free to imagine that this particular area has a surge of movement or rhythm, thus enabling the eye to travel throughout the design.

Dynamic Rhythm: This rhythm is created by a forceful element or treatment of plant material, thus creating an illusion that the design has suddenly surged into life and has become a forceful component of the real world, demanding the attention of the viewer to the point of saying, "Here I am, look at me! Question my being here if you like, but after application of the elements and principles of design, I have the right to be here." This is the concept of dynamic rhythm, exciting and new to many.

Figure 39.

The curving pieces of woody stems, interestingly grouped together, are proportionally well-balanced by the variegated ginger foliage. The plant materials are also in pleasing proportion to the container.

Proportion

Proportion is defined as a measure of comparison. We always think of it in terms of size relationship, but we will also be dealing with it as it affects color and other elements of any flower arrangement. Therefore, the key word is "relationship", since nothing stands alone. We always see things in groups that are logically related. When we see unrelated things or quantities, we become weary and confused by the conglomeration.

All design starts with space. The principle of proportion should govern the relationship of occupied space (solids) or unoccupied space (voids). We must develop a feeling for good proportion in order to organize individual materials into groups, and to establish a pleasing ratio between separate groups and the entire design. There must be a reason for putting things together, but also a degree of difference in quantity or quality, with sufficient contrast for them to keep their individuality.

To determine the size of any design, begin with the area it is to occupy. In our homes, we relate the size of the arrangement to the size of the room. In a flower show, the designated space becomes our frame of reference. We work within this area, allowing an easy margin of space all around.

One must develop a sense of proportion in selecting the right container. That old rule that we have been guided by for years, that the height of the materials must be one and one-half times the height of the container will not always apply. It is most difficult to be creative when you are guided by this rule. Actually, the color and visual weight of your container must be considered, as well as its size. These qualities should bear a close relationship to the plant material you use. Often a container is perfect for the intended design, but the niche in which it is to be placed is not tall enough for the designer to establish a good proportion. An optical illusion can be created by bringing some of the plant material down over part of the container. Likewise, if the container is too short, place it on a base or something to lift it to the desired height.

When we plan a design well in advance, it will help us arrive at pleasing proportions of color, size and shape. Separate your materials, dividing the space allotments for silhouette placement, the transitional area and the area of accelerated interest. Proper scale will control the size of each individual flower and leaf. Proportion will control the size of each unit. You might think of scale as a word and of proportion as a phrase. The design you make should be composed of appropriate words and phrases, and should, when finished, make a sentence with logic and meaning.

Balance

Balance is related to the law of gravity. Although we may not understand this force, we are all aware of its power. Without much thought, we all establish an imaginary axis and attempt to balance everything in relation to it. In any design the weight, force and interest of each placement on one side of the imaginary vertical axis is compensated for on the other side to stabilize the entire design. Each of these qualities has a degree of force and weight. Always study your material carefully and evaluate its strength, then consider its visual attraction, as it will be influenced by its environment.

All rough textures and dark values appear heavy. A lily, which is an open form, has less visual weight than an orange, which is a closed form. Any form that has a broken contour appears lighter in weight than one with a regular outline. The further any object is moved from the central vertical axis, the more it gains in visual weight.

Certain materials lend themselves to the creation of symmetrical designs. However, materials that are identical are hard to come by. Perfectly symmetrical designs must be as alike as possible on either side of the vertical axis. Creative Designs lend themselves to asymmetrical balance. The development of dynamic tension through the force of balance cannot be obtained through symmetrical placement of the materials.

Balance must be considered with the very first placement. If that placement is sturdy, poised and properly placed in a suitable container, you will be well on the way to solving many of the problems of achieving balance. It helps to have the tip of the tallest material directly over the vertical axis of the design. The line may swing out, but it should return so that its terminal is above the central axis.

Dynamic Balance: Eye movement should be dynamic, fluid, rhythmic, sometimes unexpectedly dramatic. It must cause the eye to move. Balance should be dynamic, with the force of weight balanced by the force of motion. Look for plastic organization: space activated to achieve mutual relationship between assembled units and the space that contains them all is integrated. Dynamic balance is a combination of rhythm and balance.

Figure 40.

Date palm stems and small cut gourds on wired stems are combined into an interesting design having symmetrical balance. Because of its strongly vertical character, the design has a feeling of dignity.

Dominance

Each principle of design stems from one of nature's own laws. Dominance has to do with "the survival of the fittest," the strong triumphant over the weak. History is filled with examples of nations, or groups of people, that rose to power for a brief time, only to go down to the graveyard of oblivion at the hands of an even stronger society. The battle for survival goes on all around us daily, and also within ourselves. When we are torn between opposing forces, the emotional turmoil within us induces severe nervous tension, and we become exhausted and indecisive.

Dynamic living depends on how we channel our resources and energies in a single, purposeful direction. To do this intelligently we must determine our goal, and, when confronted with conflicts of interest, choose those things that are best suited to fulfill our purpose.

Figure 41.

This design is an excellent illustration of how color can provide dominance over large forms having subdued color. The column of yellow lilies and variegated ginger foliage, placed in a blue-green container, is more eye-compelling than the two large pieces of mullein. The design is also a wonderful example of contrast of textures.

Figure 42.

A beautiful design with clean-cut lines is well integrated through a dominance of color, which is provided by the bright pink ginger blossoms.

If an artist attempts to paint two different pictures on one canvas, he will end up with two parts, but no whole. Since we cannot view the two separate parts at the same time, there is no satisfaction in the contemplation of his work. He must have one thought, one idea or one mood to create a single impression. Emphasis should be placed on what is important in the composition, and the nonessentials should be made subordinate in order to attain unity.

When this same principle of emphasis (dominance) is applied in flower arranging, a designer must start by considering the special qualities of materials. A dozen different flowers will each have some distinguishing characteristics. One may have great beauty of form; another commands attention because of its size; a third is remarkable for its color. However, if they are all to be used in a single arrangement, each must be made to blend with all the others to create a single impression. One form, color, texture or size will have to dominate. The need for a unified relationship would outlaw the haphazard selection of materials, the senseless accumulation of unrelated qualities. An understanding of dominance will determine the importance of each placement in relation to all the rest.

Dominance and unity can be established in many different ways. There is a dominance that depends entirely upon repetition. A bunch of tulips with no noticeable variation of form, color or texture can claim dominance, but offer little else. It has a "same song, second verse" quality of tiresome duplication. While there is an undeniable unity, there is not enough variety to stimulate interest. A more subtle dominance permits one quality to overpower another. Everyone likes a contest and loves a winner. Dominance has the strength to master and subordinate.

Actually, dominance is a means of simplification. Certain elements, by repeated use, permeate a composition, with each strengthening the other and achieving unity by the magic of common qualities. Dominance may be established through a single quality if it is handled expertly.

To achieve dominance of color, select a container closely related in hue to reinforce the authority of the chosen color. The dominant color must be repeated in its same degree of lightness or darkness, its same degree of strength or weakness. Once assured of an undeniable dominance, value and intensity may be changed to give variety. While unity is the goal, too much sameness is a serious fault. When the function of contrast is understood, the direct complement of the design's dominant hue may be included without threatening the oneness of effect. Properly used, contrast will be subordinated, merely pointing up and enriching dominance. We are pleased when established values, like old friends, appear and reappear, calling for no special introduction, other than friendly recognition.

You may elect to feature a certain dominant line, repeating and modifying it to establish a special style that reflects its characteristics. If the main line of a design is straight, the whole arrangement will reflect its dignified personality. Other lines may extend away from it, but as you view the whole design, the natural response is to feature the line.

When working with a dominant texture, its particular tissue structure must be felt. Thus, the character of the arrangement is set when a particular color, form, line or texture has been chosen as a dominant feature. Attention of the observer has then been focused on a particular aspect within the confines of the design.

Contrast

As opposed to dominance, contrast is not senseless contradiction, but has emphasis by means of difference. It calls attention to certain features of a design that might otherwise be overlooked. We know from the study of science that a positive electrical charge will attract a negative charge. This is the natural law on which contrast in art is based. When hues from opposite sides of the color wheel are placed side by side, each gains in importance because the difference between them is so evident. A rough texture is more conspicuous when it is placed next to a smooth texture. A rounded form displays its roundness to better advantage when contrasted to an elongated form. A straight line speaks with more authority when it dominates a curve. This is the natural attraction of opposites.

We have to learn to handle contrast well. Too much will tend to destroy unity. Complete contrast causes dissension; it is explosive and dangerous. To make an arrangement, we might take seven lavender larkspur and combine them with five lavender asters, thus repeating every quality except texture and form. We would achieve pleasant variety, but little contrast. If we use five yellow roses with the seven larkspur, texture and value would be repeated, but hue, intensity and form would be changed. This would be contrast. There would be certain likenesses, but greater differences. The rose would appear more rounded against the elongated form of the larkspur and more golden against the lavender hue. If, however, we put three red apples with the lavender larkspur, we would have dissension. There would be no relationship of form, color, intensity, value, texture or size.

In the study of color, you learn that as green paint is added to red paint, a point will be reached where color cannot be identified. Too much contrast has neutralized both the red and the green. The same neutralization takes place when acids and alkalines are mixed. From these examples, you learn that contrast must be controlled.

In a floral design, the greatest amount of contrast is used in the area of accelerated interest, where lines converge and the design begins its development. The amount of contrast depends on the size of the arrangement more for large arrangements and less for small ones. It also depends upon the style of the design. Creative designs feature the shock of contrast and, thus, have greater distinction in the proper setting. Traditional Period designs, as a rule, do not reflect a true understanding of contrast. The current trend is away from strongly centered focalization, a rebellion against over-emphasis. When too much contrast covers too large an area, the rest of the design becomes a background instead of an integral part of the arrangement.

Contrast has the power to attract attention, but not to hold it. It can be lessened by gradual transition of closely related values. The strength of contrast will depend upon the degree of change, the size of intervals. A wide interval is one that jumps in value from dark to light, in intensity from strong to weak, in texture from rough to smooth, or in size from large to small. A close interval is quite near, but not necessarily the next in scale of change. A medium interval would, of course, be a compromise between the two. The degree of contrast will depend on what you plan to achieve. Unity is more important than emphasis, and it is wise to use the spice of contrast sparingly until you learn the fine art of seasoning.

Above all, do not make the mistake of selecting a container of contrasting color to your chosen harmony. The container is not as important as the plant material, and the added contrast makes it difficult to keep the container subservient. It occupies too much space to serve as a contrast area, and its placement in the design is not appropriate.

All the principles of design are a check on each other. The contrasting direction of lines establishes balance. Contrast stops rhythm from going too far. Contrast brings dominance into sharp focus and gives emphasis to good proportion.

Figure 43.

This large design staged on the floor is very illustrative of the effects of contrast in a design. The smooth, shiny cypress knees are balanced by a large grouping of plant materials having a variety of forms, textures and colors.

Scale

Scale is known to be a measure of size. But size is a relative term. Something is large or small only when it is compared to something else. A pointed example is the circus clown dressed in a loose, full costume, with a tiny hat perched on his head: the lack of suitable size relationship between the large and the small impresses us as ridiculous, somewhat humorous, which, of course, is intended.

Since scale is intuitively apprehended, an exact definition of the term is difficult. Applied to artistic endeavor, the best that can be said is that scale is an imaginary yardstick used to bring all components into consistent and harmonious relationship in size. It doesn't matter whether scale is large, medium, or small as long as relationship remains constant. We can say that scale is an adjustment to requirements. A large room requires large furniture while comparatively small furnishings are suited to a small room. A little chair fits a small child; an adult is more comfortable in a larger chair. We learn from nature that it is the fitness of things that is at the root of scale.

A three-inch arrangement staged in an eight-inch niche would be dwarfed to insignificance. An arrangement that is too small or too large for its niche is faulty in proportion to its environment. When the scale of things in combination is visually satisfying, they will appear their true size, neither dwarfed nor enlarged.

One sees how closely allied are the principles of scale and proportion. But the two terms are not synonymous. Scale refers to the individual units in a composition, proportion to the areas the units occupy. This is size adjustment between the amount of one element or one area to another. The size of a flower in relation to a container is scale; the area or amount of plant material to a container is proportion. Pleasing scale relationships usually result in a composition of good proportions. Good proportions reveal a relationship of measurements according to scale.

The arranger understands all this to mean that there is good scale in a composition when there is a visually satisfying relationship in the size of the individual units to each other, to the whole design, to the environment, and to the human figure. In view of this, he has been taught to assemble the units in a rhythmic sequence of large, medium and small. An adjustment in size of units one to another and to the whole can be diagrammed as follows:

- Large, medium and small units represent a rhythmic relationship of sequence, a grade series. This exemplifies unity within variety, a worthy quality in well-designed composition.

- A small size would lend refinement in addition to completing a rhythmic sequence, a series.

- The jump for the eye from the large to the comparatively small unit registers them unharmonious; the eye sees no relationship of size. Introduction of a medium-sized unit would supply transition between the large and the small, thus creating a recognizable sequence in size.

- A large unit would aid in eye appeal and complete the series in graded relationship. (At least three units are required in a rhythmic sequence.)

Figure 44.
This lovely rhythmic design shows skillful handling of scale. All components are pleasing in comparative size-relationships to each other, while employing enough variation in scale to avoid monotony.

Design is not an accomplished fact. It is not a formula to be memorized. Rather it is an activity, a doing. From the first selection and placing together of materials, we seek rhythmic relationships, transitions and interest. As we work, a unifying structure gradually emerges, which is one and inseparable with the form. Techniques, procedure and general visual reaction can be taught as established facts, but this is only a small part of designing. Knowledge alone will not create a work of art. It must be guided by intent and imagination, and this process cannot be taught. *To design is to bring orderly form out of chaos.*

Neither formula nor rule can be given for design. A design must grow naturally, guided by intent, selectivity and limitation of materials. Basic principles of design can be learned, but they will never give the complete answer. Principles are tools of expression, just as words and sentences are the tools of literature. With practice, the use of the tools become intuitive, and the designer becomes a creative artist.

CHAPTER FIVE

Traditional vs. Creative Design Concepts

Introduction

Line: Line designs are those in which the linear pattern is dominant. These arrangements are characterized by restraint in quantity of plant material used and by an open silhouette.

*Line-Mass:** Line-Mass designs are those designs in which additional plant material enhances and strengthens the line design. The silhouette is open. This design is very adaptable to the contemporary home.

Mass:

TRADITIONAL MASS (Period Designs): a grouping of plant materials placed in containers that were typical of the period, such as urns and vases of alabaster, metal, silver, porcelain or glass. The shapes of these designs were either round, oval, circular or triangle in form. Plant materials were loosely distributed throughout the design, never grouped together as to types or kinds.

*Mass-Line and Line-Mass are terms used synonymously.

Figure 45.

The circular container and gracefully curved wood establish the dominant line, and are enhanced by strelitzia blossoms and variegated aspidistra leaves.

Typically, certain flowers and colors were used for each of the designated periods. Each recorded period had specific hallmarks and characteristics that distinguished designs made during that time era. The designs were used as decorative compositions, created to enhance areas of homes, churches or public buildings. Mass designs are characterized by the use of a large quantity of plant material. The plant material is not crowded, but the design has a closed silhouette. Distinction depends on the grouping of forms and colors.

MASS (Mid 20th Century): Mixed garden-type flowers, as well as greenhouse-grown and flowers from tropical areas of the world, were used and often combined. Often only one or two types of flowers were used with foliage. Dried plant materials were often combined with fresh plant materials. This design is usually associated with the type of designs that were created by American florists and garden club members during the 1950s and 1960s. Traditionally, massed forms were usually used, with additional forms and lines added. It was during this period of floral art that the Line-Mass design was developed and shown, combining the mass of Occidental designs with the emphasis on line of Oriental designs.

In evaluation of any design, we will find it is either Line, Line-Mass or Mass in concept, depending upon how much material, what kind of material, and how the material is used. We must be guided by hallmarks of the two divisions of design:

Figure 46.

Line-Mass designs, whether traditional or creative, have an open silhouette with plant materials added to strengthen and enhance the line.

TRADITIONAL and CREATIVE

These hallmarks differ, and we must understand these differences in order to properly classify the design. In order that we may have a better understanding in our design analysis, the characteristics of Line, Line-Mass and Mass are listed. The foremost characteristics found in these designs are discussed. Some may have similar characteristics; some may have none that are similar. However, this will enable one to see a difference in the three types of guidelines, without always being governed by rigid, set rules. Remember that whatever art is, it is not a science, so, therefore, cannot be judged by strictly formulated rules.

Figure 47.

For Mid-20th Century Mass Designs, arrangers grouped and mixed one or two types of garden and tropical flowers with foliage, in a closed silhouette.

Traditional Designs

Traditional Line:

- Restraint is shown in selection of garden-type flowers and/or foliage (one or two kinds).

- Naturally linear materials with slight enhancement by flowers and/or foliage.

- Excessive grooming helps to make line more dominant.

- Line is never painted or treated, not even dried materials.

- Radial placements are the dominant method of organization.

- Harmonious color harmonies are chosen, often tints rather than pure hue or shades.

- Line direction is often vertical.

- Basic, plain simple containers are selected.

- Lines of materials never cross.

- One point of emergence is employed.

- Accessories are often included.

- Bases are often used.

Figure 48.

The naturally linear heliconia stem and strelitzia leaves, chosen and used with restraint, emerge from one point to form a strongly vertical Line design.

Traditional Line-Mass: The Line-Mass is a combination of both traditional line (Oriental) and traditional mass (Occidental). Often Line-Mass designs are created and placed in traditional settings. When this is done, flowers in keeping with the period are used and colors are chosen to blend well with the surroundings. These designs are placed in reproductions of period containers that are in keeping with the surroundings.

Figure 49.

The eucalyptus line is strengthened by the addition of snapdragons, carnations and the elegant butterfly accessory.

Traditional Mass:

- Period containers typical of the era are chosen.
- Assortment of garden-grown flowers illustrative of the era are arranged according to the specific style for a period.
- Arrangements are usually more decorative than expressive.
- These designs are usually a combination of spike, round and spray-type flower forms.
- Colors and combinations of colors depend upon the period of the design.
- The total form is usually oval, circular or triangular.
- There are no crossed lines in the placement of materials.
- Manner of placement (looseness or tightness) depends on the period.

Figure 50.

An antique pink glass compote holds flowers of varying forms, sizes and soft pastel colors, all combined in a traditional Mass design.

Creative Designs

Creative Line:

- Radial placement of plant materials is often used; however, materials may come from different areas in the container or from behind wood or other objects, such as plastic, rocks, wood forms, etc.

- A focal point may be developed.

- Bolder, larger flowers and foliages.

- Unusual, often shocking, color harmonies.

- Line directions are often diagonal or horizontal, as opposed to the predominately vertical directions of traditional designs. If vertical direction is used, it is forceful and direct.

- Lines may cross to create areas of tension within the design.

Figure 51.

A Creative Line design uses clipped dried palm leaves to establish a forceful horizontal line direction, enhanced by the single pink ginger blossom. Leaves are looped around the container in a creative manner. Since a majority of the materials have been abstracted by changing their natural appearance, the design could also be classified as an Abstract Creative Line design.

- Dried materials are often painted or otherwise treated to create a forceful impact.
- Man-made materials, such as plastic, metal, glass, wire, can be used as the dominant form if the schedule does not prohibit their use.
- Plant materials can be shaped by the designer to create unusual effects.
- Plant materials may be placed out of water, if needed, to create dynamic force within the design.
- Dried and fresh plant materials are often combined for unusual effects.

Creative Line-Mass: All the characteristics given under Creative Line designs are followed, with the exception that more materials are added along the linear path of the line materials to create more of a massed effect (focal area) at the mid-section.

Creative Mass Designs: The following guidelines will characterize the Creative Mass design concept.

- Containers are used that are considered to be creative: multi-opening, forceful, big and bold in form, color and texture.
- Plant materials that may be new to the viewer may be used: distorted forms of dried or fresh materials, unique fibers or wood. Common materials are used in unusual ways, often combined with tropical, exotic materials.
- The silhouette (outline) is closed, avoiding a dominant radial placement of materials (which has all materials coming from one area in the container).
- Grouping of like kinds and types of materials together (in the same area), as opposed to the scattering of materials as found in Traditional Mass designs.
- Dynamic, dramatic features of natural or carved forms, such as figures of animals, birds, people, etc., are often used.
- Open spaces are included within the design's form, while the silhouette is still closed, creating a different and unusual massed effect.
- Designs may be of any form; however, basic traditional geometric forms of circles, ovals and triangles are avoided. Elongated, exaggerated forms are best. Stylized forms are created by combining forms, overlapping forms and using parts of forms in different ways.
- Combinations of fresh and/or dried plant materials are often used.
- Painted and treated dried plant materials may be used.
- Interesting forms of wood, vines, palm spathes, etc. are often combined with other plant materials.
- Groupings of plant materials in multiple containers, such as used in Synergistic Designs, may be used as examples of Creative Mass Designs.
- Some of the large floor-type designs created by the Japanese Masters could be listed as Creative Mass designs.
- Designs should be large in size, using quantities of plant materials.

- Creative Mass designs may have some abstract qualities, such as distorted forms, bent lines, trimmed foliages or shaped plant materials.

- Plant materials having lasting qualities may be used out of water for unusual design effects.

- Creative Mass designs may be vertical, horizontal, diagonal or of any shape. However, shapes with traditional characteristics, such as formal balance, should be avoided.

Figure 52.
Creative Line-Mass designs have all the characteristics of Creative Line designs. More materials have been placed in the central area of the design to create a massed effect.

Figure 53. (Opposite)

The container's multiple openings permit insertion of areas of grouped materials; the open spaces within are defined, keeping the outer silhouette closed.

Abstract Creative Designs

(*Editors' note:* Abstract Creative Designs are discussed in more detail in Chapter 7. They are summarized briefly here as they relate to Creative Designs, as a whole.)

Abstract Creative Line:

- Most abstracts are basically composed of linear materials.
- Lines may be painted or otherwise treated if dried, and if the schedule does not prohibit.
- Lines may be either geometric or free-form, as long as the design requirements are met.
- Lines may cross for forceful effects and with purpose.
- Lines may be abstracted by nature or shaped by the designer, but should be bold, direct and free from confusing details (removal of excess leaves, crossed smaller branches, etc.).
- Creative Abstract designs may be totally composed of line materials.
- No focal point is ever developed in creating an abstract design; interest is equated throughout the design with the eye moving through and around the entire form.
- Radial placement of plant materials is avoided, as this creates a focal area where the eye will be directed to the container or holder of the materials.
- Creative containers with many openings are usually used, in order to place the materials in striking and unusual positions.

Abstract Creative Line-Mass: All the characteristics given under the Creative Abstract design are followed, with the exception that massed areas of flower forms are placed throughout the design to create areas of interest, which will cause the eye to move from point to point through the design. Placement or development of any area that may cause one area to be focal is to be avoided. We look *through* abstract designs and look *at* traditional and conventional designs.

Abstract Creative Mass: Many contend that there is no such thing as an Abstract Mass design, because if we use space as a positive and open up the abstract, there can be no massed form. However, the creative artist can create a massed abstract. This can be done by color, texture and form in selected plant materials. A closed silhouette can be created, which is the main characteristic of all Mass designs.

Creative Vertical Designs: In a Creative Vertical Line or Line-Mass design, the dominant thrust of the design must be vertical. There may be more than one point of emergence, and more than one focal area if this does not destroy the vertical thrust. When Creative Vertical designs are shown in a niche or against a background, the dimensions of the niches or background should have greater height than width.

The vertical form of design is one that can express many variations of creative inspirations. The creative process is indeed working when we take a basic pattern like the vertical line, and by experimenting with different types of containers and materials, we can make this design one of beauty and excitement.

Vertical – Perpendicular, or at a right angle, to the plane of the horizontal: upright; straight up and down; at a right angle to the plane of the supporting surface; upright position; applied to that which rises in a straight line with the plane of the horizontal.

Perpendicular – the preferred term in geometry; refers to a straight line forming a right angle with any other line or plane.

As the vertical line is a force from point to point, moving the eye up and down, the design should always be defined within a vertical volume of space, such as a background or open background frame, etc. When this is done, the vertical is better defined. Otherwise, if a vertical design is placed on a flat, open-topped table for display, and the design penetrates an open volume, its force is diminished greatly. Some are under the impression that vertical designs can only be made in one manner. This is not true, as the creative process allows us many variations.

There are two principles of design in particular that control Creative Vertical designs:

RHYTHM and **PROPORTION**.

Rhythm – Continued eye movement through a design is defined as rhythm. The rhythm may be abrupt, straight, actual. If so, the rhythm is quick and

---

Figure 54.

A Creative Vertical Line design need not be abstract. This combination of bold colors, forms and textures gives a strong upward thrust to a design, having a new look.

factual; this, of course, is the main characteristic of vertical movement. However, we are told that we need contrast of line, so slight interruption of movement can be that added touch needed for Creative Design. This interruption can be accomplished by using contrasting forms of line. However, if the dominant directional movement is still vertical (after adding these), then the design is still considered to be vertical.

Proportion – Proportion applies not only to the design, but to its staging. Measurements must include the container's measurements in establishing the design's height. The old measurement of one and one-half times the height of the container often will not work, because in the creative concept of design, exaggerated lengths of material are often desirable. Materials can often be two, three or even four times the height of the container, depending on their size, color and visual weight. For instance, we know that a thin, light, airy line of plant material can be placed much higher than a heavy, dark piece of material. We must remember

Figure 55.

This design's strong rhythmic line is created by the antler, with contrast provided by the clustered white tulips and the open, airy bear grass.

that even though these two principles are considered the leading principles in creating a Creative Vertical Design, all principles are governed by all elements. The principles of contrast, dominance, scale and balance are equally important to design success.

Containers – Any type of container may be used in creating a Creative Vertical design, even a horizontal container. Materials (vertical in character) must be thin and tall, and rise vertically from many areas of the horizontal container, with space intervals between the materials, thus moving the eyes away from the heavy horizontal form of the container. Forceful contrasting colors should be used to take emphasis from the heavy container's form.

Creative Horizontal Designs: In a Creative Horizontal Line or Line-Mass design, the dominant thrust of this design is horizontal, although absolute horizontal placement of all materials is not required. Balance is created through the use of unlike forms, sizes, colors, etc., and is usually asymmetrical. Eye movement through the design is in one direction and may be more easily achieved with informal balance. Contrast of line, form, color and texture play minor roles in Creative Horizontal designs. If shown in a niche or against a background, use approximately two-thirds of the space. The horizontal dimension of the niche or background should be greater than the height.

Figure 56.

In a Creative Horizontal Line design, absolute horizontal placement of all materials is not required. Balance is achieved by careful placement of a combination of unlike forms and colors.

Defining Space in Creative Design

Recently a friend and I were standing on the back porch of my newly-purchased plantation house, which stands on brick piers six feet tall. We were admiring the picket fence that had just been installed surrounding the back area of the house. My friend stated very innocently, "Isn't space wonderful and exciting when it is defined?" The statement started my mind into a creative process of designing. So, in turn, I would like to share some "space thoughts." His statement was most fulfilling, since we had stood in this same spot many times in prior weeks trying to establish what should be done with this area. Once the fence was installed, it was easy to visualize what else was needed and how we could obtain the end result. You perhaps are saying, "What does this have to do with flower arranging?" I might answer this by a simple statement of one word: *Everything!* Until the 1960s, we were concerned with space as being related only to the principle of proportion (the area in which the design was to be placed). However, when we freed our thinking with creative concepts, we realized that there was a hidden force working within the design that was controlling everything we did. Only then did we start talking about space. It was during this era that space was added to the list of elements of design.

Figure 57.

Space is defined in and around this Creative Design, with voids providing depth by a see-through effect.

In traditional use of space, consideration of the area where the design was to be displayed was of first and utmost importance because it determined the amount of materials we were to use; the form of the total design and its dimension demanded certain textures and colors, as well as consideration in other areas. We were taught that voids (space volumes) at the outer areas of the design added interest. We were then told that we could control depth with space. Space became more and more important as we ventured into creative designs. Then came **abstract** designs. Our thinking broadened, and we realized for the first time how important space was as a major element of design. We then began to define space within and around the design. It became a working force with which to deal.

The traditional design forms are space forms (the circle, triangle, etc.) that are filled with plant materials, whereas abstract design absorbs space as it contributes to it. Space exists in all dimensions. Space carries and is carried by all design elements, and we look through abstract designs instead of just at them.

Space shapes can be, and often are, the most dominant feature of any abstract design. These shapes are no longer empty voids doing nothing within the design. They are charged with interest through forms and direction, and their message can overpower that of solids within the design. In other words, a spiral vine is not only a solid line, but also a solid line twining around space! However, the space areas must be of varied sizes or the spiral will become a static formal force.

The creative designer does not dare leave the distribution of space to chance, but must use it knowingly, not negatively but positively. Without the variety, contrast and organization of directional movement of spaces, the solids, receding and advancing colors and textures, a design can become lifeless. There are several ways we can utilize space: by *enclosing* space within the design's form; by *absorbing* space into the outline of the design; or by *penetrating* the design with one or more volumes of space. Space works upon its own entity. In other words, we do not have to place plant materials in an enclosed space volume to point it out and make the viewer aware of the volume. Space should, and can, speak for itself. Properly placed, it will work for the design every time. The clever designer can and will have complete control of space within the composition.

Space in a design frees the viewer to use his or her imagination to supply the details. Space within the form, as well as surrounding it, can suggest abstract ideas and emotions. Space (its shape, direction and intervals) can control, slow down or activate the visual rhythm through a design. The creative designer usually uses space wisely to increase and enhance rhythm, thus establishing unity more quickly.

The shapes of all spaces, as well as the masses, should be varied and interesting. Monotonous (even) space intervals usually result in sluggish, dull rhythm. Space rhythms differ in variety and speed. Some rhythms are sharp and staccato. Some are smooth and even, some make us seek and reach for balance. Each design with interpretive character will demand different spatial rhythm.

If we are using space as a material item, then we must subconsciously consider it a visual solid form. It is most important that any plant materials used in an abstract design must be in scale with the volumes of space that are used. The same consideration should be given regarding proportion. Space, shapes and forms carry with them certain psychological communication. Listed below are a few:

- *Cube* . . . weighty, steady.

- *Circle* . . . completion, unity.

- *Cone, triangle* . . . precision, balance.

- *Horizontal oval* . . . quiet, restful.

- *Slanting oval* . . . instability.

- *Rectangle* . . . stability, strength.

- *Straight angles* . . . masculine.

- *Curved areas of space form* . . . feminine.

There is another dimension of space: that which is found naturally in plant materials, such as leaves with natural holes and decorative wood with natural spaces in its form. These are often used, as well as those areas of space that the designer creates to add interest to a design, and their consideration is important to an end result.

In summary, space is not only considered as the area in which a design is placed. In abstract designs in particular, there is a hidden force found in its use that will activate a design when it becomes a forceful element. Think space, use space, and by all means, define it, because when it becomes defined, its force becomes evident to all who take time to look.

Creative Staging

In the past, the background was a passive color and/or texture placed behind a design to add complementary or contrasting color sensation needed to complete a design. Its control by the arranger either added to or detracted from the finished product. Background sizes, and sometimes colors, were given in the schedule in order to achieve uniformity in class staging. The designer was required to stay within the dimensions listed in the schedule and was not allowed to have any part of the design touch the background, or to attach any components to the background. The creative process in design has made the background an active part by incorporating it into the design in many ways. The form of the background may be something other than the rigid elongated rectangular form of yesteryear. It may take on any form that may contribute to the design: triangular, circular, vertical, oval or other combination of shapes desired (always controlled by the schedule's wording).

The design may extend beyond frames, backgrounds or boxes if these are incorporated into the design and if the design does not go outside the total space allotted. The schedule must state if these are to be "incorporated into the design." When the schedule states the design will be exhibited/staged "against a background" or "within a frame or background," all components must be within that frame of reference.

Figure 58.

The coils of rope and edges of the leaves incorporate the frames by bringing them "into the picture," the opposite of using frames or any other staging device as a frame of reference.

Materials (plant materials and other components) may extend above, or beyond the background in any direction; they may enclose, surround or penetrate the background. This process is called incorporating the background into the design. Following is a list of the different ways in which we may incorporate frames, backgrounds and/or boxes into a design:

- Raising the frame, background or box off the table top, going around, over, above or under with line materials.

- Placing one or more containers in front of, behind, above or below the background, then adding line materials or flowers to incorporate the frame, background or box into the design.

- With frames and boxes, materials and/or containers, accessories may be attached to the front, back or side or placed on top of the structure (depending upon its construction).

- Backgrounds, frames and/or boxes may be combined, presenting unusual areas where containers and/or materials may be placed to create unusual effects by adding concealed lights in the total effect.

- Incorporation may be achieved by repeating colors, textures and forms found in plant materials into the colors, forms and textures of the frames, backgrounds and/or boxes.

- To incorporate is to "bring into," so this demands that we do more than just place materials beyond the confines of the frame, background or box.

- Never forget that we are doing Creative Designs, and our limitations are only hindered by our abilities. Learn to try new ideas with your medium (plant materials), and be totally happy in and with what you may attain by trying.

Figure 59.

Most Creative Designs stage well on pedestals, whether free-standing or with a background.

Figure 60. *(Left)*
A large, dramatic design is staged on the floor and also includes a background.

Figure 61. *(Below)*
A dynamically rhythmic design consists of gourds, with a small pineapple used for interest and contrast in texture. It is staged in a niche of neutral color.

CHAPTER SIX

Other Creative Design Styles

Assemblage

Ralph Mayer, in his *Dictionary of Art Terms and Techniques*, defines Assemblage as "the technique of creating three-dimensional works of art by combining various elements, especially found objects, into an integrated whole; and a composition so constructed." An Assemblage may be either free-standing or mounted on a panel, and may include elements painted, carved or modeled by the artist.

Mayer further defines Assemblage in *The Artist's Handbook of Materials and Techniques* as being "an art form in which the artist finds or selects an object, then mounts and displays it in such a manner as to exhibit its aesthetic qualities of form, contour, color, texture, etc., as though it were a creation he had formed himself."

When such objects are more or less two-dimensional, such as paper items, and are pasted to a flat surface, the work would be called a Collage. When the objects are definitely three-dimensional or mounted or joined together with other objects, especially when free-standing, the work is called an Assemblage, usually with the French pronunciation. These "found-objects" are usually man-made; their quality is best if enhanced by age or weathering; and they usually are displayed without being altered in any way. A mass-produced item exhibited for the same or similar values is called a "ready-made".

The display of such objects is a 20th Century art form, practiced by the Dadaists and Surrealists. The objects may be given a new aesthetic quality by inventive methods of mounting and display. The artist's role in presentation is creative in that it points out aesthetic values the object already possesses, which were not deliberately considered in its construction. The concept of the "found-object" is in accordance with a Surrealistic doctrine that holds that anything with aesthetic value, even inadvertently so, is a work of art and worthy of being exhibited as such.

William Seitz, in *The Art of Assemblage*, defines Assemblage thusly:

- Predominantly assembled rather than painted, drawn, modeled or carved.

- Entirely, or in part, the constituent elements are natural or manufactured materials, objects or fragments not intended as art materials.

- Objects are grouped not by function or emotion, but by size, color, form, etc., conveying the real spirit of design.

"Found-objects" are any of various objects or materials picked up by chance and incorporated into a work of art. Assemblage guidelines:

- Materials are of non-art type—"bits and pieces."

- Abstract rules apply in placement of components selected.

- Space is used positively.

- Dynamic impact is essential.

- If man-made bits and pieces are selected and are of greater volume than the plant materials, it is suggested that Assemblage classes should be listed as eligible for the Designer's Choice Award. If the "found-objects" are used in a minor role, such as a line within a design of plant materials, or objects placed at the base of a design of plant materials, this is then classified as an arrangement with accessories, which would not be considered an Assemblage. The secret lies in a factual statement in abstraction, governed by abstract guidelines.

- The Assemblage must contain some plant material, if it is to be classified a flora design.

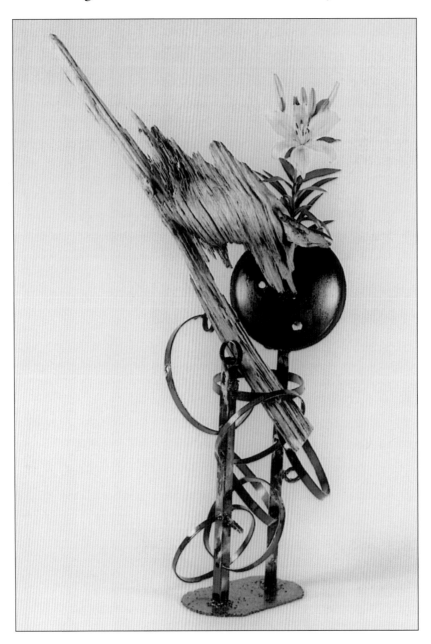

Figure 62.

"Found-objects" are non-art ready-mades, usually used without alteration and displayed to exhibit aesthetic qualities of form, color and texture in Collage, Assemblage, and sometimes other Creative Design styles.

Collage

The word "Collage" comes from the French verb *coller* (meaning to paste, glue or stick) and the Greek verb *kolla* (meaning to glue). When we apply this art medium to flower arranging, the arranger must combine plant materials that are light in weight and have a lasting quality, with other two-dimensional materials (paper, fabric, etc.) to a flat surfaced, sturdy background. The plant materials used must be dried thoroughly and pressed flat before using.* Collages differ from the traditionally constructed plaques, which usually employ radial placement in their construction, and are composed of three-dimensional objects in a traditional concept of design. Collages should not be confused with Assemblages, which are composed of three-dimensional objects or with seed pictures or mosaics, which are craft work.

Any two-dimensional material may be used, and as one progresses in the area of Collage, a visit to art shops will present many new and exciting materials that one may use. However, a fine basic Collage may be done with little investment.

It is the illusion of depth that is required in Collage work. This is achieved through selection of proper materials, proper organization, placement of materials on the panel, treatment of color, and by the adding of shading and depth through different media. If one is unable to obtain the desired effect through the use of paper and plant material, such materials as gesso, plaster, sawdust, sand, woodshavings, etc., can be used. Also, unusual effects can be created with use of paper, by tearing, cutting, peeling, layering, painting and burning.

(**Editors' note:* Fresh plant materials, if they are flat ones, may be used as well. Use of "found-objects" is now optional in Collage.)

Construction

A "Construction" is a form created from a limited number of kinds of materials (no more than two). The materials may be either plant materials (such as wood, cattails, yucca or other material that will have a lasting quality even when used fresh and not placed in water), or man-made material (metal, wire, plastic, glass, wood, etc.). Upon completion, the form is usually geometric in feeling and has a strongly architectural look. If the form is constructed from man-made materials, plant materials, either fresh or dried, must be added to qualify the design as a flower arrangement. The plant materials may be placed within the confined frame of the Construction, or may be added to extend above and beyond the limits of the Construction to give the design needed height or width.

The Construction may be presented as a free-standing form, or may be placed on a base. The constructed component may also become the dominant form within a design by being hung onto or placed beside a container. However, when this is done, the container must be used as a design component, serving as a form of color or as a base for the Construction, and should never be dominant. Construction is often confused with Assemblage. They are different in both concept and execution, even though each may have qualities found in the other.

Figure 63.
Palm spathes have been fashioned into a Construction in an excellent example of plastic organization. The other plant materials add beauty without detracting from the sculptural effect of the Construction.

Duo-Design

A Creative Design placed in one container with each side (front and back) of the design being different is termed a "Duo-Design." The front side is one design, while the back is another design. The design should be placed where it is free-standing and can be viewed from each side. The Duo effect is obtained by either painting dried materials, with a different color used on each side, or by placing a large form in the center of the design that will prevent seeing through the design. If the latter is done, then different materials may develop the center of interest on either side. When judging this design, it is suggested that the designs be placed on table tops or on pedestals, allowing access to both sides and permitting both to be seen. Each side becomes a different class to be judged. This prevents constant turning of the design or moving from side to side to evaluate the design, resulting in an innovative design having two sides that are to be evaluated. Therefore, the design might possibly score high on one side and receive a lower score on the reverse side.

Figures 64 and 65.

The two sides of a Duo-Design are shown. The design is created in one container, by one designer, with the front and back being different from each other.

Both designs share one spectacular piece of wood as the primary line and are separated by a large dried leaf, which screens the design on the front side from the one the back. Large yellow proteas are used on one side, while the opposite side uses orange pincushion proteas and strelitzia.

Framed Spatial Design

A Creative Design is designed as a single unit, suspended in a frame-type structure. The design embodies lightness and airiness, and is usually an unconventional use of plant material and/or other components. There is no actual motion: movement is implied. The design should appear to float like a frozen sculpture in a volume of space, defined by the frame. Materials should be placed to provide a visual penetration of the framed volume of space. The design should not be confused with Mobiles or Hanging designs.

Kinetic Design

A Kinetic Design is one in which there is actual movement, or the appearance of movement is dominant. This movement may be motorized, induced by air currents, or implied.

- A *Mobile* is a grouping of freely suspended forms having visual balance. It depends on air currents for actual free movement.

- *Motorized designs* are those with programmed or motorized movement.

- A *Stabile* is a static sculptural form, fixed in position at the base, which implies motion.

Mobiles are abstract, three-dimensional sculptures having movable parts that are set in motion by currents of air. The Mobile, a comparatively new creative art form, was invented by Alexander Calder in the early 1930s. He is the originator and master of the form. Anyone who is really interested in Mobiles should study his work. Any time any art form is expressed in an entirely different medium, adjustments and allowances must be made. In flower shows, Mobiles must be suspended from above; at eye level is a good position. Use of plant material is a must. Dried flower, leaves, reeds, grasses, bark, seed pods, driftwood, branches, vines, etc., are possibilities. Fresh plant material, if used, gives added weight along with the mechanics to keep it fresh, and that weight must be compensated for. Staging becomes a problem in many flower shows, and consideration should be given to the location where the Mobile class can be staged. Total staging, with reference to location, how to be hung and the color of the background against which the Mobile will be seen, should always be considered and noted in the schedule.

Mobiles can fill a horizontal or vertical space. Technical balance is not the only requirement. Space, form and color equal balance. All elements and principles of design, guided by abstract hallmarks of design, should be considered. Repetition of forms, colors and strong textural contrasts are recommended. Also consider the rhythm of movement and the changing of the entire form by reflective light. The closer the arms come to one another without touching while moving, the more interest and excitement will be created. A Mobile should appear to be floating weightlessly. It is important that Mobiles move easily and readily.

Motorized Designs are designs with programmed or motorized movement. There are two types of designs in this classification listed below:

- A design placed on a turntable, on which the entire design rotates. Careful consideration should be given to these designs in both the placement of all components and the speed at which the turntable rotates. Components should all be anchored securely in order for the design to remain intact as long as the design is on exhibit. The continued rotation may tend to loosen plant materials that are not anchored properly. Speed of rotation: the rpm (speed) of the turntable or motorized base should be of a speed that would allow the viewer to adequately view the design. In order to evaluate a design, the interplay of components must be seen without confusion. The speed should be slow and gradual, and as the design turns, the placement of materials gives changing picture planes that will excite the viewer.

- A static design with a motor concealed in the container or with other mechanical aids: certain plant materials are attached to the motor and a portion of the design moves. The *entire* design does not move. A pinwheel within the design, having a small concealed electric fan to induce air currents, would fall within this category.

Stabiles are sculptured forms suspended in space, motionless, but giving the illusion of movement while being anchored from below to an immobile base. The Stabile, like the Mobile, is a term invented by Alexander Calder. The Stabile remains still, having no moving parts, yet is not static. It looks as if it could take off in flight or move in some direction. They are compositions portraying arrested, imminent or implied motion through optical illusion or darting eye movement.

Figure 66.

A Stabile gives the illusion of movement. The viewer feels the strong rhythmic lines of the twisted, but vertical, vine carry the eye out into space. The neutral pottery container is hardly noticed, but it does reinforce the idea of a space ship due to its form.

The suspended form may be vertical, horizontal or diagonal; but must have thrust that will carry the eye out of the design into space, causing activation of the element of space within the design's frame of reference. The Stabile may be free standing or three-sided, but must have depth. The dominance of weight is at the top of the design, away from the base or standard that holds the design aloft. The standard, or line that anchors to the base, should not be static in any form or position, but should have such dynamic force in its form or placement that this contributes to the overall design's form. The base, standard, stem or pedestal is never dominant and sometimes can be almost concealed by being the same color as the background.

Op Art

Op Art, called Illusion Art, is a term first used in New York in 1963 for a style of art in which sharp-edged abstract patterns stimulate a reaction on the retina of the eye, producing an illusion of dazzle or movement. When colors other than black and white are used, the dazzle effect is enhanced by the juxtaposition of complementary colors. Op Art is a style of completely non-objective art, lacking subjective message. A methodical collection of geometrical patterns using bright colors, it features lines, angles and forms (basic shapes). The optical illusion is created by close juxtaposition of geometric forms and the use of strong color combinations that force darting eye movement, qualifying these designs as a form of Kinetic design. For the Standard Flower Show, Op Art is a creative design having implied motion. Op Art fabric, paper, plastics, or forms may be part of the staging or of the arrangement itself.

Reflective Design

Reflective is a Creative Design that contains some components that involve the viewer through the use of reflection. There is a personal sensation created by optical communication between viewer and design. Reflective means to give back an image, to throw back. This is not a design placed in front of a mirror.

Any reflectant material used should provide an illusionary concept. The surface quality of the reflectant will influence the design's effectiveness. Subtlety is achieved through dull or shaped reflectants, vividness through shiny surfaces. We are all familiar with natural reflections occurring in nature; still, dark bodies of water create the best true reflections. However, abstract qualities of reflections can be obtained from mountain streams, or wet surfaces of rocks, slate, coal and other hard-surfaced natural materials. With proper lighting conditions, certain plant materials take on a reflective quality. Man-made materials respond to light more quickly, giving an instant reflection. Chrome from the auto parts store; brass; fiberglass; glass; silver; copper; bits of mirrors; metallic papers, e.g. giftwrap; "wet" paint (looks "wet" when dry); and aluminum foil are examples.

Figure 67. (Opposite)

The shiny brass forms reflect light, involving the viewer and maintaining interest. The structural clarity of this design has great impact.

The designer must read the schedule carefully before creating the design. He or she must be careful of the amount of reflectant used and how it is used. Since Reflective designs are Creative Designs, the amount of man-made reflective materials should not be restricted by the schedule. All requirements for Top Exhibitor Awards are specified by the schedule, so always read the schedule carefully.

Sculptural Form Design

Sculptural Form Design is a three-dimensional Creative Design, either pieces of one type of material fastened together to form a single unit, or naturally formed as a single unit, having the effect of sculpture. The dominant sculptural form must have the appearance of being carved, chiseled or welded together. Three-dimensional quality is of prime importance. Examples of the above:

- One type of material fastened together to form a single unit: for example, take several pieces of decorative wood that are alike in form and color and fasten them together, creating one form out of the several pieces. Other kinds of materials may be used in the same manner.

- Naturally formed as a single unit: for example, one piece of decorative wood that appears to be a completed sculptural form. Single units of other kinds of materials may also be used, of course.

In both cases, additional plant materials should be added to complete the design, but the sculptural form itself is of only one kind of material. The form to be used may be of decorative wood or any other dried plant material, as well as any type of fresh plant material. Other possibilities are man-made materials like plastic, wire, metal, glass, styrofoam, rope, etc. However, the award requirements will determine what combination of materials may be used.

Guidelines:

- Use restraint in selection of materials.

- Use materials (fresh or man-made) that can be easily shaped, and will hold their shape when formed.

- Be selective in choosing a base on which the Sculptured Form is placed or anchored.

- Make sure that the form is three-dimensional.

- Select and carefully place additional plant materials to the Sculptured Form. Dominance of the form must be maintained; do not destroy its effect by adding too much additional material or by the placement of these materials. Supplementary materials are intended to serve as *enhancements* of the Sculptural Form.

- The form should be free from confusing details; therefore, remove any obtrusive side branches, etc. Make the form look like it has been sculpted from the chosen medium.

Figure 68.

A gigantic piece of weathered wood is a magnificent natural sculpture. It is the Sculptural Form in this design. Its smoothly textured form is enhanced with two creatively grouped placements of plant material.

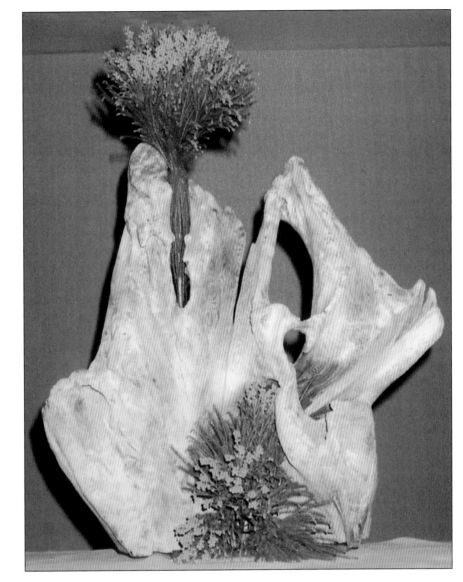

- Containers are not usually used in Scuptural Form designs unless the container *is* the Sculptural Form. In that case, care would need to be exercised to assure that additional plants materials would enhance the Form, but not dominate it. This is an example of when it is permissible for the container to be the dominant component within the design.

- Such things as completed sculptures, figurines of people, animals, Madonnas, etc., are allowed in a Sculptural Form design. When they are used as the Sculptural Form, plant materials must be used to enhance the overall design.

Still Life Design

A Still Life Design consists of a group of inanimate objects organized by the artist according to some theme; these are either symbolic (expressionistic) or merely aesthetic (decorative). The theme is usually carried out by the objects that are chosen, which may be man-made or natural forms (such as shells, minerals, horns or bones, etc.), realistic, functional, decorative,and/or utilitarian.

Defined words in the above statement:

- **Functional:** of or pertaining to a function or functions; designed for, or adapted to, a particular need or activity.

- **Utilitarian:** pertaining to, or associated with, utility; stressing the value of practical over aesthetic qualities.

- **Utility:** the condition or quality of being useful, or being worthwhile.

- **Tradition:** the passing down of elements of a culture from generation to generation.

- **Realism:** in general, the depiction of human figures, real objects or scenes as they appear in nature, without distortion or stylization.

Still Life Guidelines:

- Objects selected are art type (decorative), functional, utilitarian.

- Traditional or realistic placement of objects is used.

- Development and story-telling is found in the objects selected.

- Realism is evident throughout the entire design.

- Usually displayed in a niche or against a background.

- The story is told more with objects than by arranged plant materials. If the objects are used in a minor role, such as a line within a design of plant material, or if objects are placed at the base of a design of plant material, this is then an arrangement with accessories, and cannot be called a Still Life.

- Must contain some plant material to be classified as a floral design.

Stretch Design

A Stretch Design is a Creative Design using two design units placed in a given area, alike in color and/or texture. One part is smaller in size and appears to be a portion of the larger design that has pulled away. Strong line materials are used as a connective between the two designs. The effect is that of a total design that appears to have had a small portion of the larger design stretched away from the larger arrangement.

Figure 69.

A Stretch Design requires two units, the smaller of which appears to be a portion of the larger design that has pulled away. A strong connective line joins the two.

Transparency Design

A Transparency is a Creative Design that includes see-through parts that permit some components to be viewed through others. One dictionary defines transparency as "when light rays are used so that objects on the other side of an element may be seen distinctly." Another's definition is more detailed: "That which is transparent, as a picture or other matter for exhibition; made upon or behind glass, thin cloth, paper, porcelain, or the like; intended to be viewed by the aid of light shining through it, hence, a framework covered with thin cloth or paper bearing a device or devices for public display and lighted from within."

To understand Transparency, one must also understand the word "transparent," which is having the property of transmitting rays of light so that bodies can be seen through; so loose or fine in texture or open in mesh that what lies beyond is not concealed; sheer, gauzy; as a transparent fabric or yoke. Supplemental lighting enhances the transparency effect.

Figure 70.

In this Transparency Design, the color impact of the gladiolus is subdued, and the viewer's interest is piqued by the see-through effect of the seafan. This design also incorporates a reflective disc at the top of the design, which would also create sound if the disc were struck. The design could also be classified as a Vibratile, incorporating reflective and transparency qualities.

Underwater Design

Underwater is a Creative Design with parts placed underwater to create interest. Water magnifies the materials, creating an element of interest and surprise. Scale must be given consideration when selecting plant materials. The forms of material, when placed underwater, show more clearly in clear or transparent containers.

Plant materials having hard surface qualities should be used, as these will not deteriorate rapidly when submerged. Evergreens, tropical flowers and foliages are suggested. Materials and mechanics are magnified when the container is convex, so care must be taken to see that mechanics are well hidden, and that the plant materials are magnified; this is the purpose of placing plant materials under water. To avoid air bubbles in the water, first place the materials in the container, then add water.

Figure 71.

When a part or parts of a design are placed under water, the magnification adds surprise and interest. Mechanics must be carefully handled, with meticulous workmanship to prevent floating debris.

Vibratile Design

Vibratile is a Creative Design incorporating sound. The sound is induced by placing components, such as horns, bells, windchimes, whistles, etc., within or next to the design. The viewer is expected to be drawn into the design by participation. The viewer touches the design or device (object used to create sound) to cause a stimulus. The touching will create a sound by vibration. This sound is a part of the designer's concept of creativity. This new form of viewer participation demands study and thought. The sound-maker device must be an integral part of the design, not just an after-thought. In theory the device should be placed in the design in such a way that it becomes a part of the design: a form, color, texture, etc. Designs and sound-making devices must be so anchored that the viewer may touch without disturbing the design. The sound makers should not be obtrusive to the point of annoying others who might be in the exhibit area.

(*See Figure 70.*)

Figures 72 and 73.

Synergistic Designs are Creative Designs having three or more units with common characteristics, with each unit usually being incomplete in itself, but serving as part of an artistic combination that result in a complete and cohesive design.

(*Editors' note:* Over the years Bob Thomas introduced a number of new design styles at his *American Guild of Flower Arrangers* seminars (e.g. "Creative Spiral," "Satellite," many others). Only those officially approved by the NCSGC Flower Show Schools Committee have been included in this book.)

CHAPTER SEVEN

Abstract Creative Design

The Nature of Realism

"It is the task of art to express a clear vision of reality." This statement by the painter Piet Mondrian gave rise to thinking on the question of what in art activity constitutes an inherent connection with the real. The credo of the sculptor Constantin Brancusi states, "Simplicity is not an end in art, but one reaches simplicity in spite of oneself by approaching the real meaning of things." In these declarations and in voices of other artists proclaiming or implying like-sentiment, the term "real" (reality or realism) refers more to an artist's inner vision, developed through observation and translated into form, than to subject matter.

Stimulating things have taken place in contemporary art, not the least of which is a projection of reality beyond the visible material things into "the soul of man's mind." This points clearly to the dictum of Leo Tolstoy: "Art is a vision of emotion." Alas, there are few arrangers among the many who acknowledge the wisdom of this axiom, and yet, it explains a broad and deep concept of what is real and true in art expression, one we call "super-realism."

Figure 74.

An inner vision has been expressed by selection of components having expressive character. The design incorporates minimal abstraction.

Work in which the arranger has failed to push beneath surface quality for expressive character gives evidence that she or he experienced no personal reaction to the subject: the spiritual reality is missing. Even though a consequence may hold appeal for the eye, it is an uninspired performance. Nothing is communicated to the viewer that is not already known.

The theoretical basis for this subjective and newer concept of realism came into being with the setting into motion of abstract art in 19th Century Europe. Creative artists accepted abstract theory as a means of expressing their inner visions, thereby, stretching the truth of reality beyond the sphere of sight and into the realm of the spirit.

The question for arrangers is how does this serve floral art? Habitually, realism has been a catch-all term for all representational art, so one wonders how the arranger can pierce the visible to expose the invisible in order to enlighten, strengthen and convert life experiences into the higher order of reality and truth.

Probably, if a poll were taken among devotees of flower arrangement, a majority would maintain that realism is found only in a composition in which the finished structure is likened to observed visual data: something one sees, has seen, or could see with the physical eye. Distinct from *subjective* expression that transfers into form the arranger's inner senses, the *objective* variety, expressive of naturalism, may seem unpersuasive or unconvincing to some.

At the inception of flower arranging in America, attention was directed toward decorative design, with plant material used in its natural pattern of growth. Later when a subject of actuality or idea was interpreted, the arrangement was narrative or illustrative in character. This, too, was arranged in a naturalistic manner. In these early stages of floral art, adherents were content to follow this direction without question. Their work, both decorative and narrative, satisfied its purpose, often with richness and grace.

Because in floral art these traditional practices are close to common experience, there is no need to offer examples. It is enough to be reminded that both types represent objective expression. But likeness to natural appearances is too simple an aim to bring forth creative work; imitation kills the germ of creativity.

Some may protest by asking, "Are you saying that arrangers should refrain entirely from portraying naturalism?" The answer is an emphatic, *"No!"* While raising a point of progress in arrangement, it is not suggested that *all* naturalistic facets should be avoided. What should be made clear is that *dominantly* naturalistic arrangements often show little or no creativity. Let it be remembered that for the most part, the decorative and narrative works of tradition are repetitive and imitative, usually not creative. The very nature of such work makes it impersonal, for it gives form to sight impressions only. Imitation does not show inspiration, and inspiration is needed to stimulate a creative work of art. It is activation of instinct causing feeling that produces this stimulant.

Definitely, the point at which a creative arrangement grips the heart and mind of the audience is the point at which a work departs from details of appearance to present (not *represent*) a personal reaction. The purpose of the arrangement should determine which level of reality will dominate, and therefore characterize, the work. Objectivity or subjectivity, natural or abstract, if you will, is a designer's choice.

Figure 75.

In Creative Design, the arranger goes beyond the natural and decorative, showing originality instead of repetition.

The thing to keep in mind is that the contemporary creative arranger may, and probably will, include certain traditional gestures and symbols in a composition. Work that excels will not be a collective expression by any means. On the contrary, when personal concept is the leading attribute, the completed arrangement shares with the viewer the artist's feeling at the time the design was created.

In regard to the use of symbols, a word of caution is needed. Be sure symbols are universal, not completely private, because the viewer will reject the too private symbol as unintelligible, and this would stifle communication.

The difference between natural realism and super-realism could be explained as a difference between perceptual and conceptual approaches to arranging. The perceptual aims at pleasing the eye. The conceptual has a spiritual vitality that is more moving, due to deeper involvement with other senses: the inner world of man, we can say. Natural reality and super-reality imply two ends of a scale that might exist between them. The skillfully balanced blend of these outer and inner factors creates a well-founded fusion of forces in man's inner reality and in the environmental reality surrounding him.

When presenting an interpretation of a specific subject, heavy emphasis is placed on a reasonable personal reaction to that subject. The arrangement furthers the creative realm. Picasso's early paintings, for example, document this. Creativity lies in *super-realism*—in realism that can be felt.

Nature is the best teacher where art is concerned. This is probably responsible for a popular dislike of abstract art because things appear different from the way the physical eye sees them. "They're not real," many say. But commitment to this mode of thinking is too limiting to an understanding of reality. There is no denying that objective expression (naturalism) comes close to common experience, but, as it has been pointed out, it excludes the most vital part of realism, that personal domain of the spirit. For this very reason, the work denotes a lack of disciplined intensity; it seems commonplace by comparison. What we must focus on is that super-realism strengthens the validity of arrangement as a fine art.

Figure 76.

Natural reality and super-reality are skillfully blended
in a fusion of forces having dynamic impact.

Enough of theory and on to practical application. To carry out the intended message by means of arrangement, the first consideration is selection of plant material. Here, knowledge of abstract art is brought into play. While abstractionism is opposed to naturalism, it is not opposed to nature, as is generally thought. In fact, nature in the guise of super-realism characterizes the whole phase of modern art. Paul Cézanne speaks to this in a winning way: "Art is a harmony, parallel with the harmony of nature." In so saying, Cézanne was not thinking of surface features, but of sensations he received from nature (the cylinder, sphere and cone phenomenon, for instance); not a copy, but a harmony of relationships between outer and inner realities. Thus, he gets underneath the surface of this subject to convey what instinct tells him is the essential character, and therefore, possesses design potential.

To essentialize in this way, the arranger must learn to envision the medium not as specific plant material, but as colored and textured shapes, lines and forms, each having a life of its own. As every word spoken excites a stirring within the listener, so likewise does every object seen by the viewer. This hints at an ancient animistic way of seeing objects, believing they have a spiritual life of their own.

Figure 77.
The plant material was envisioned as colored and textured shapes, lines and forms, each having a life of its own. The form created by alternating reversed stems of broccoli is a particularly creative useage of plant material.

"A rose is a rose is a rose." We are indebted to Gertrude Stein for this poetic phrasology. It can be interpreted to mean that in a work of art, the rose is something more than merely a rose. The inability to perceive our medium as more than flowers, leaves, branches, etc., is a stumbling block to progress in the art of floral design. However, the problem grows easier if we will come to grips with the fact that we actually see objects as abstract shape, line, form and color before we identify them as tree, flower, cloud, etc. When the eye focuses on a chrysanthemum, for example, we see it first and primarily as a colorful abstract sphere. Only after this do we see its exciting surface display. This is where a penetrating vision shows its tested effectiveness. Through seeing deeply, we perceive the intrinsic spirit of components, their life quality or essence. This is what makes a component what it is, apart from its appearance.

By seeing deeply, the artist becomes aware of an emotion filtered through observation and association, stored in memory. Super-realism is colored by the way one's life has been molded, by what one knows and experiences of many and varied principal traits of objects seen singly and in relationship to each other. Obviously, the outcome is a diversity of new images through a combination of previous experiences. In this, the creative power of the imagination is exercised. The mind perceives imaginative images as reality. It is imaginative concept that supplies vitality to the elements of a design. As applied here, vitality does not, of course, have reference to animation; it refers to a spiritual inner life, the inner force and energy that are attributes requiring adjustment within the entity of the arrangement. We may conclude that the elements will have importance only in so far as they contribute to the general effect.

Closely allied to essentializing or distilling is translating what you see into imagery that accords with your personal feelings. Art historians call this "shaping the emotions." Since this shaping process varies according to one's experiences, we should be true to ourselves and not undervalue our reasonable emotions. The resultant work is subjective expression that gives *form to feeling*. As inner vision, it may well appeal to all the senses. The feeling that wells up in the artist is, perhaps, the most persuasive property of fine art expression.

Deductive reasoning brings realization that super-realism in a well-executed personality-directed composition adds up to a lot more than structural form, which is more than the totality of its parts. We discover that it embraces three significant factors, abstracted from three sources: from nature in a collective sense (external); from instinct, sensation and feeling (inner life); and from technique (elements taking place in their own vocabulary of shape, line, form, etc.). In art, form known as "non-objective" is a good example of the latter. It is so named because the artist eliminates subject matter altogether:;there is no subject apart from the composition itself.

Figure 78.

The components work together to create a vital, rhythmic design, giving life and impact to it.

Interest here is not abstract art in its own right, but rather as it has entered the floral arrangement field; therefore, it is imperative to call attention to a current error in terminology, which is a reference to abstract work as "non-real." This unfortunate label is prompted, not so much by lack of subject matter, as by a rather common idea that shapes and forms of design elements are generalized, and are thought of without reference to details in individual situations. In abstract concept, the opposite is the case. Each is accepted as a precise and specific detail item, functioning not only for aesthetic value, but also as the basis of perception. Because of a deeper way of looking at the same set of facts, the elements emerge in composition as an outer expression of the inner life. This being so, non-objective arrangement is not an escape from reality, but is a penetration into *super-reality*, capable of evoking feeling, probably an unexpected feeling, in the viewer.

What can be said of color in connection with super-realism? Chromatic color especially affects our emotions directly and immediately, so it is a most important ingredient. It gives fullest impact to expressive meaning by suggesting or recalling impressions associated with differing hues. Just as shape, line or form are chosen without regard for what they actually are, the same is true of color. To help channel feelings and moods into an art form, use color for its own particular force, not in the natural but in a design relationship. This centers on images of color unlike what you see, not represented as they appear to the eye. In the interest of super-realism, the combination of elements is intended to convey subjective meaning, and color composition ought to effect a definite key tone: light or dark, warm or cool, bright or somber, etc., depending upon the previous message.

Figure 79.

Chromatic color affects our emotions directly and immediately, suggesting or recalling impressions associated with differing hues.

Lack of space curtails discussion of the special dimension of color symbolism. Should this be an unfamiliar topic, research of color symbolism will prove to be invaluable.

To assure satisfaction within Gestalt psychology, the artist-arranger builds a design on a personal concept of the problem, though the mind is set upon that which changes not—namely, the governing laws of art principles. However, these principles need to be reexamined and reexperienced if harmonious relationships of elements are to convey emotional meaning. Harmony, we know, is a common attribute in all good design. To achieve it, giving birth to an art form consistent with an artist's insight, necessitates the governing principles working together in what can be called "process of growth." This infers a gradual development of one part to another. One part will suggest another, and the design will grow out from it.

In assembling the elements in such work, the mode of organization must not bind the artist's inner impulse. Therefore, technique is not controlled by traditional linear perspective with one center of interest serving as a magnet of unity. Instead, oneness is gained by a number of interest areas being equated or carefully balanced to form a well-unified whole over which the eye travels without obstruction. This will be recognized as plastic organization, a method for attaining order introduced with the advent of abstract arrangement, and one that is essential for achieving *depth* in a design. It is worthwhile to note that, in this case, operational elements are distributed so that they are somewhat isolated in space, not compacted as in traditional order.

Figure 80.

Operational elements are distributed so they are isolated in space, not compacted as in traditional order, thus demanding a new way of seeing.

Figure 81.

Dark and light, warm and cool, mass and line submit
to a rule that is wholly aesthetic within the creative concept.

The change in attitude and technique we have considered influences the viewing public, and certainly the critic and judge. It stimulates a fresh approach and appreciation, although, to the uninitiated, it may tax understanding. Many still are too apt to think of arrangement as a preconceived art form instead of a structure of organic growth in which subject-matter has planted just the seed. An even greater burden is placed on the observer, for the viewer is expected to participate more than ever before. So, just to be appreciative of an arrangement, or in judging, to adequately evaluate the work, the viewer must detach himself from what the subject is about. Discriminating perception comes not from seeking out what the work represents, but from what it makes the observer feel.

What is Abstract Creative Design?

The full values and forces of this art in flower arranging take not only many hours of research, but also hours and hours of actual work to create, and to understand. At the very start we have a strong critical prejudice from the majority of arrangers, saying, "I do not like it." With this criticism in mind, let us try to open the door of creativity for those who do not understand, or want to understand this form of 20th Century art. Flower arranging is an art, and an Abstract Design is a visual symbol of the 20th Century. We must give it a place, along with the many other systems of design, in our knowledge of floral art.

The strongest criticism of Abstract is a response from the masses that it is "ugly". Many things may be great works of art, and yet appear ugly to those with limited or possibly romantic standards of beauty and taste. We Americans tend to surround ourselves with beauty, think beauty, live beauty, and at every chance, create beauty. Through the power of observation we can, through our abstract art forms, see beauty that we had never seen or given a thought to before. When it comes to real beauty in abstract art, time will probably outstay us. It is a fine experience to feel beauty, and we cannot have too much of it, but don't dismiss everything outside your educationally conditioned, personal conception of it. Many people were educated to believe in nothing beyond a romantic pleasure in art, so that the sense of the infinite escapes them completely.

There has always been some form of two-dimensional abstract art, but such art in the past was intended to ornament buildings, clothing or household goods rather than to communicate ideas and feelings, or as in the case of the printed page, to set out in a way that was visually effective, ingredients whose meanings were wholly symbolic. In tile or mosaic, jewelry, textiles or pottery, repeating patterns or symmetrical designs were used decoratively and symbolically as part of larger artistic or purely utilitarian purposes. Among familiar things, only certain Persian carpets and woven rugs are a close parallel to abstract paintings, having, as they do, delightful qualities that transcend good craftsmanship and pleasing decoration. No doubt in Islam, where portraying a human likeness was forbidden, the shape and color of abstract symbols acquired a greater acceptance, achieving a richness and variety parallel to natural forms.

Only in the 19th Century did popular taste demand that the surface imitation of natural objects should become the sole standard of skill. However, throughout history we see the dual nature of the artist's activity: at the same time, as he represents the objective world, he is busily making a composition in which dark and light, warm and cool, color, mass and line submit to a rule that is wholly aesthetic. Out of dislike for this rigid 19th Century thinking came the revolt that founded abstraction. Two-dimensional artists as well as sculptural artists devoted themselves to the understanding and study of this new way with art. During this movement, our Western interest in flower arranging was born, and like other artists, we followed strict rules for many years. Then we, too, found that we were not satisfied with technical procedure in creating our designs. A new way with our medium was developed, as we studied written words and proven works of abstract artists.

Abstraction is not a temporary phase or a fashionable fad, but an essential part of the new tradition and the new culture that we are creating. Abstract is not a "Movement," as opposed to Realism or Expressionism, for these are complementary attitudes. It is not escapist. On the

Figure 82.

Abstract art is indeed similar to music, as it has freedom from the confines of the real world. It is purely art for its own sake. The wood in this design was abstracted by nature, while the palms were clipped and shaped to complement the wood's form.

contrary, art that does not mirror contemporary life, but alters and reshapes it, in some sense, becomes the most creative and realistic of all. The living art of every age is a part of our endeavor to dominate or transcend circumstances. Abstract art, in its truest sense, is completely disengaged from the visual appearance of the objective world. Many of its supporters contend that it is similar to music, since it represents or imitates nothing of the natural world. For this reason, it is considered absolute and pure.

The American Heritage Dictionary defines Abstract as "the concentrated essence of a larger whole; to take away, remove; to consider theoretically; to think of a quality or attribute without reference to a particular example or object: considered apart from concrete existence or a specification thereof." Abstract Expressionism is a school of painting that flourished after World War II until the 1960s. It was characterized by its emancipation from traditional brush-work, in freely developing shape in design by its exclusion of representational content. Abstraction is the act or process of separating the inherent qualities of properties of something from the actual physical object or concept to which they belong.

Abstract designs are a break from naturalism, the result of the artist's expression, in which plant material and other components are used solely as line, form, color and texture, incorporating space to create new images. The designer uses the elements in a new manner to communicate with the viewer. All components need not be abstracted; however, the overall design must be an abstract concept. If a component can be identified as a flower, leaf, branch, etc., the identification has little or no importance in the finished design.

Abstract design emphasizes the use of space and depth, and of areas of tension. Interest must be equated throughout the design. Design components are generally bold in form, size and color; however, delicate forms and colors may also be used successfully in abstract design. Gradation of size and color are ignored, as are set patterns and set combinations of components. The use of unexpected color combinations and the combination of components not usually associated with design, together with possible use of exotic plant materials, play an important part in the creation of abstract designs.

The container used in abstract designs may be an integral part of the design, but need not be subordinate to plant material and other components. Containers used for abstract designs usually have multiple openings (all openings need not be used), and other non-traditional qualities.

The pattern and form of plant material may have been altered by wind, plant diseases, etc., distorting and changing its natural appearance. The designer may abstract plant materials by various means, such as clipping, stripping, bending, tying, folding, or any other means of manipulation. Color and texture may be altered, unless the schedule prohibits the treatment of dried plant material. (Fresh plant material may not be treated.) There may be unconventional use of man-made materials found objects.

Abstracted plant materials and other components are usually placed in a non-traditional manner. Plant material may be placed upside-down, side-ways, hanging, moving, clustered to create new forms, etc.

Abstract design has:

- Abstraction of some or all plant materials

- A non-traditional container

- Interest equated throughout, established through areas of tension

- Emphasis on an interpenetration of space

- Little or no radial placement of components

- A dominance of abstract characteristics

There are two categories of abstract design: those that are *expressive* (subjective, having a title or theme to be interpreted), and those that are *decorative* (non-objective, having no theme or title).

Figure 83.

Aspidistra leaves and palms have been clipped to abstract them. There is beautiful compatibility of colors and textures of components, resulting in bold, strong and dynamic forms.

How to Achieve an Abstract Creative Design

Abstraction is a concept that is unreal to us. To abstract is to change naturalism as we find it and know it into an unrecognizable line, shape or form. Texture and color change of materials can alter their representational appearances. For complete abstraction, abstract the materials, abstract the overall form of the design, and arrange in a non-conventional container.

- Select natural abstractions, which can be found in nature. Wind, water, or plant disease malformations can distort plant materials and change their normal appearances.

- A color change of dried plant materials can vary their normal appearance, abstracting by color unreality (schedule to govern). Painting, dying, bleaching, etc. can change the nature of these materials.

- Textural change by painting or treating can vary the surface quality of materials.

- Position and placement of plant material in an arrangement can abstract it from its normal or realistic presentation.

- Use of a non-conventional container will assure the design of certain qualities of abstraction that cannot happen when a traditional container is used.

- Placement of materials should be done in such a way that one must view the entire design; space is used as a design element in a different way. Materials are "opened up" so that one looks *through* the design rather than *at* the design. The container is used as a component of the design, a form, color and/or texture being fused into the design. Materials are not placed in a radial position as in conventional designs, but are placed in such a way as to suggest movement through dynamic tension.

- Strong emphasis is placed on space. Think space, making its use dominant in the design.

- Select bold, strong, dynamic forms.

- Keep the design simple. Pure design must evolve without being overdone.

- Use dramatic designs, emphatic lines, strong structures and silhouettes.

- Discover and utilize unusual textures.

- In using color, select the brightest hues. Avoid shades whenever possible.

- Avoid development of a focal area. Areas of interest are created by plant material and color, but a traditional focal area is never used.

- Use of a neutral or earthy-toned containers can avoid competition within the design, but striking colors colors and glazes can also be effective in Abstract designs.

Products of industry can be used, but whenever you can find materials in nature with which to create unusual effects, use them. We are flower arrangers. Yours is the opportunity in abstract floral art, as in all the arts, to discover beauty where no one found it before, and to express it with any material of your choosing.

■ To you, the *arranger*, is assigned the task of winning acceptance for this dynamic form of floral artistry, through study, experience and creation.

■ To you, the *judge*, continued study and knowledge of these new forms will help in making evaluations and decisions on the flower show floor.

■ To you, the *viewer*, comes the simple pleasure of discovery, the unveiling of newness, and the fresh recognition of wider horizons.

Figure 84.

Often unusual and exciting forms are found in nature. Whenever such natural materials can be found, they lend themselves to highly creative designs.

Summary of Understanding Abstract Design

Regarding the understanding of abstract application to the medium of floral design, beauty, in the Greek or Renaissance sense, is not the aim of abstract theory. Between beauty of expression and power of expression, there is a difference of function. The first aims at pleasing the senses. The second has a spiritual vitality that is more moving and goes much deeper than the senses. Because a work of art does not aim at reproducing natural appearances, it is not, therefore, an escape from life, but may rather be a penetration into reality: an expression of the significance of life, a stimulation to greater effort in living. Influences of other art forms (arrangements we have seen in the past) are not always direct or precise. A painter may be influenced by a sculptor, a writer by a painter, a sculptor by a painter, an architect by a sculptor, or in our case, any of the above, as well as by the Master Painter and Sculptor of Nature, with Whom we so closely relate.

It is perhaps not necessary to observe further that our art is a highly contagious "disease," and our eyes feed unconsciously on whatever formal motes that come our way. To strive to avoid being influenced by the work of one's predecessors or contemporaries is neither possible nor desirable, all questions of traditionalism apart. Artists confront their destiny with a certain unity, through the general history of the civilization of which they are a part. They react to this common destiny with a certain uniformity. We do not need a theory of dialectical materialism to explain such an obvious fact. But within this general historical process, there are complex variations that arise fundamentally from the differences in individual psychology, from difficulties of communication, from physical variations of all kinds. To distinguish between general influences and personal indebtedness in any particular case is almost impossible.

Multi-sensory Conceptions (Lights, Sound, Motion)

Vision in Motion—A Fourth Dimension: In this age of speed of which we are a part, vision in motion is a challenge of the day. This is no less so in artistic endeavor. It is revealing that artist George Rickey should state, "The artist finds waiting for him a subject, not the trees, not the flowers, not the landscape, but the waving of branches and the trembling of stems, the piling up or scudding of clouds, the rising and setting and waxing and waning of heavenly bodies, the creeping of spilled water on the floor; the repertory of the sea, from ripple and wavelet to tide and torrent...."

Indeed, for artists, vision in motion, real or imaginary, has become the fourth dimension. The natural consequence forces us to ponder the moving eye. Fast moving vehicles of transportation supply opportunity to see more than in the past; we see still objects in quick succession as well as things in permanent motion, as a fountain or waterfall. Thus, we become accustomed to seeing things in a moving field of relationships. The art revolution manifested in the 20th Century *"isms"* paved the way toward new dimension of space-time motion, in a static plane or in the shallow space such as supports three-dimensional flower arrangement.

Although the sphere of visual experience has been enlarged through science and technology, practical application in flower arrangement has remained, for the most part, fundamentally unchanged. Arrangers may be little informed of basic principles of vision in motion; they are unaware of its significance. There is need for sensitivity toward this fourth dimension if living quality is to mark our work: a vitality that compels our attention, claims our sensitivities, moves our imagination and expresses our thoughts and inclinations.

Frank Pepper, in his book, *Origins and Developments of Kinetic Art*, traces the handling of movement in visual arts back to 1860, so the rendering of motion in art work is not a new practice. In the past, artists expressed the passage of time with such things as double images, dated objects, or with something out of its historical period. But today, creative artists, fully aware that everything possesses energy to exert a force within itself, employ techniques and devices that give an expression of suggested motion to the expanded world of physical forces. This enables them to create the impression of movement in a still composition. What is new today is realization that time and space are closely united in conveying motion or a sense of motion.

As for actual movement, one example will suffice: the Mobile. This art form utilizes the medium, not in mass, but as sculpture having relationships and interpenetrations as carriers of movement, so that the viewer experiences vision in motion. The motion is unpredictable, for it depends on unpredictable natural forces, such as air currents or heat waves.

Also, there are works in which actual movement is predicted and controlled by the artist. Among this type are electric- or battery-powered compositions and mechanical hand-operated devices. By such means, movement can have pendulum swing or action up, down and around. Both space and time are involved.

Some aspects of movement are only potentially realized, not actually visible to the eye. This is illusionary (virtual, phantom) motion, movement only "in effect and essence." History furnishes us with examples. In the recorded works of Cubists and Futurists, with new knowledge, these artists pushed on to newer worlds in painting and sculpture. In spite of the simplicity of their techniques, their works revealed new space, time and motion experiences by bringing into play more than meets the eye: in many cases, a totality of the senses rather than just that of sight.

But, probably, it is the work of an artist who was neither Cubist nor Futurist that definitely and completely released artists from the traditional concept of repose, the static, and replaced it with that of motion, the dynamic. In Marcel Duchamp's *"Nude Descending the Staircase,"* planes were overlapped several times in sequence to express in this painting more than one movement in a given moment. Painters apply to such creative experience the phrase, "an encounter." Indeed, through deep and penetrating vision, Duchamp had an encounter with his subject of objective reality (the lady) and an idea (moving down the stairs). Involved are both space and time with illusionary movement in still composition the result. Stimulated by this specific means of recording a sense of movement, the viewer recreates mentally and emotionally the original moment of descending the stairs.

Illusionary movement, being only imaginatively visualized, may be baffling unless one has learned to perceive its reality through other senses, not just by sight alone. Illusionary movement is then difficult to understand only if the motion has to be perceived, as in a Cubist painting that presents objects as if the viewer were moving around them. The effect of motion in an arrangement is gained with an overlapping of planes, arranged so that each plane is behind and above the others; leaves handled in this manner are especially appealing. An important detail is the distance between the overlapping components, which must be short enough to span the gap between the overlapping elements. It must be short enough to span the gap between the planes, and yet, the elements (leaves, in this example) are seen as moving in a smooth and pleasing continuity.

Psychologists tell us that buried within a deep dimension of our being are feelings aroused due to associations related to the elements of design. Because everyone experiences the same reactions when confronting line, shape, form, texture, color and space, the elements are accepted as universal symbols. To use Carl Jung's phrase, they represent the "collective unconscious" dimension of mankind's experience. To thoroughly understand this, it is necessary to examine *optical* (vision), emotional (feeling) and *kinetic* (motion) characteristics. Among ways to do this, there are four deserving of special recognition:

INSTABILITY . . . TENSION . . . EXPLORATION . . . VIEWING

Instability is expressed through the use of elements in unstable positions. A pyramid standing on its point or a mass suspended in space without support are examples of shape and form. Movement is a matter of feeling as well as of seeing. The eye does not necessarily follow direction of shape or line, but a movement is realized in a specific direction when we feel a proper relationship with other elements. To see it and feel it can be different experiences, although they are not necessarily separate operations. There is also the need to take into account characteristics associated with the elements. For example, think about line. In the diagonal, we see and feel motion where there is none because common to the image is seeing and feeling—a gradual increase in obliqueness from the vertical to the horizontal, to which humans are oriented.

In addition is the association with running man, slow in movement compared with that of a bullet's path. The sense of slow or fast motion depends on the artist's control; the degree of slant he gives to the line is a determining factor. The character of the vertical line is related to the force of upright growth and is associated with standing man, making it a symbol for steadfastness and strength. The horizontal direction, unless exaggerated in a design, is related to reclining man, symbolizing peace and tranquillity. On the other hand, an overemphasis of the horizontal in a composition is associated with streamlined vehicles, suggesting speed.

What is said of direction of line is applicable to shape and form as well. Closed forms can be grouped into masses, and the shapes given any direction desired. In doing this, the important thing, as it is with line and form, is that the resulting shapes be thought of as more than just elements of design; they must become elements of construction. Perhaps, an example in arrangement is helpful: the Stabile. In this still composition, elements are coordinated in a sweeping pattern, anchored lightly, not heavily, at the base. In no way can the pose of a well-executed Stabile be static, for its components are subtly combined to imply illusionary motion; it seems on the verge of actual movement. This phantom quality can be strengthened if the pattern of the Stabile's background is blurred in effect.

Let it be repeated that the artist's problem is to involve his intellect and his emotion, so that he both sees and feels the elements in meaningful relationships. Learning to do this is not difficult because everyone has an inherent capacity to develop inner perception through penetrating vision, a function discussed in a former chapter. As with all illusionary motion, participation, as well as imagination, is required of both artist and viewer. The resulting impression is that Stabile and viewer are moving in relation to passive objects around them.

Figure 85.

Shapes and forms, as well as directional lines, share importance in the success of this dramatic design.

Tension, one of the dynamic properties in art, is another technique for directing sensory impact by suggesting motion. Tension has always been an integral factor in art expression, but today, in order to vitalize compositions and, thereby, give them the quality of living art, it is planned and controlled by the artist. The arranger will do well to reinvestigate the knowledge of tension. He will recall that a vital ingredient is *opposition*, which habitually is defined as contrast. Opposition is all important, for, as in the physical world, there is no movement without gravity or friction, so, in art expression, there is none without opposition. Gestalt psychology explains why this is so: it is a matter of balance, for the desire for symmetry and stability inherent in man drives him to balance mentally all unequally distributed masses.

We can draw an example from early training in the art of flower arrangement: an area of space on one side of a composition's vertical axis can balance a mass or form on the other side. The reason is that within the whole design, each unit releases a certain amount of energy, thus bringing equilibrium by means of counter-poise and counter-weight. Dynamic spatial balance, the consequence, is like the balancing movements of the human body—right leg and foot forward, left arm and hand behind. What happens is that an activating force within each element (including areas of space) exerts a pull from the axis or center of each, causing the eye to move up and around, establishing tensions. The stronger the pull, the more vital is the tension. The arranger's problem is to place each unit in relation to the pull it exerts on every other unit. This is truly a creative act.

Color tension should not be overlooked. A few tips that have proved to be beneficial follow:

- Fluctuation: the moving back and forth between areas of intense and clashing hues

- An area of grayed hue in relation to an area of intense value of the same hue

Figure 86.

Tension, one of the dynamic properties of art, is a technique for suggesting vitalized motion, as shown in this Botanical Design.

- Grayed hue of a background repeated in the center of an arrangement

- The dominant hue in the design's foreground repeated in the background

- Hues in different planes repeated in triangular pattern in the body of the arrangement, and related to pull the eye from foreground to rear, to left, to right, from base to tip

Exploration refers to a third way of vitalizing an arrangement through illusionary movement. This embraces attention-getting controls effective in both types of order used in flower arrangement: traditional and plastic organization. In the traditional, one main center of interest serves as a pivot of unity, with the eye carried to the design's highest area, where it is easily released and drawn back to the center of interest to begin exploration again. Eye passage through the composition is thus prescribed. Plastic organization is directed toward an unprescribed eye passage: the eye is free to roam from unit to unit, one as important and interesting as any other in the totality of the design. Meaningful relationships establish the all-important unity.

Common to both orders is the need for something to attract the viewer's attention—something of shock value is ideal. This might be satisfied with the current passion for "see-through" plant materials or transparent objects, or reflections on polished or mirrored surfaces. Translucencies that combine both color and light are a challenge. In explorative technique, perhaps light is the most valuable attention-getting tool. Experienced arrangers are aware of the effect it has on tactile quality in changing the structure of an arrangement. Interception and transmission of light, depending on direction of the light

Figure 87.

The pussy willow stems provide a see-through effect, while calla lilies comprise shock value.

shining from above or below, from the side, in front of, or from the rear, fuse elements together or break masses into smaller areas. With proper coordination, these offer vision in motion. A very strong attention-getter is light from a key-hole fish light or emitted from a special device, manipulated within the arrangement itself. The cold light of luminescence, manually or electrically powered, works much like Rembrandt's painted images that appear to emanate from the composition. It seems to be almost a source of light, not just reflected.

Flower arrangement, in the same way as other visual arts, has its inherent laws through the structural use of its own medium. When an arranger is not concerned about what plant material is like in its natural state, he can apply the possible wealth of distorted shapes and forms to add varied space directions to further illusionary movement. Dimensions and properties can be overemphasized, as well as supply convex, concave, geometric, free-forms and other shapes. But it must be repeated again and again that distortion is an enriching aid only when it is employed with reason.

Unfortunately, these suggestions for attention-getting controls give nothing more than brief explanation of their influencing function toward illusionary motion. A point of great importance should be emphasized, that in order to create virtual motion, all must be considered with an eye for tensional balance.

Figure 88-A.

Illusionary motion is a matter of feeling, as well as of seeing. Placement of the large variegated philodendron leaves provides tensional balance within the design.

Viewing, a fourth means for vitalizing arrangement through illusionary movement, affects those who view the completed arrangement. When certain relationships are achieved within the work, a sense of motion is increased for the viewer. For instance, curved surfaces at different heights appear to move as the viewer alters his position of observation; the arrangement is animated simply by walking from side to side before it. A stroboscoptic effect results by shifting position before a mesh or grid screen behind which an arrangement is staged.

As we think on these topics, it becomes clear that space, time-motion and other processes for achievement cannot be fully evaluated without knowledge of rhythm. In obtaining coherence of the whole, there must be rhythmic movement from one area to another. Arrangers understand the technical conception of rhythm, so there is no need to dwell on it.

A significant fact is that rhythm suggests the elemental force or energy of nature. In fact, dynamic symmetry, the basis and rhythm of natural growth in plants and animals, is a study in "motion experience," as scholars define it. What arrangers must keep in mind is that space-time motion can be enlarged upon through thoughtful handling of rhythm; space is activated by a dynamic constructive rhythm of elements.

Figure 88-B.

Placement of rounded, curving forms increases the sense of motion, as well as providing several different areas of tension, thus equating interest throughout the design.

Let us summarize some of the most significant points we have considered: Illusionary (virtual or phantom) motion is the action of forces embodied in line, shape and areas of color and texture by direction or position in relation to each other. With freedom from the static, fixed structure of the past, relationships designate a new dynamic and kinetic existence in our work.

The key to it all is a relationship that touches the very heights of fine art. Breaking away from conventional vision, the arranger views his subject or subject theme in a simultaneous act of seeing, thinking and feeling, so that he can coordinate the visual symbols in proper relationship. Sometimes totality of the senses is involved, but one thing is certain: that the creative act, without exception, uses more than just the intellect. This is to say the creative arranger conveys a sense of motion where there is none, through a synthesis of the intellectual and the emotional, by bringing into play penetrative seeing, thinking and profound feeling.

Kinetic art, simply defined as "moving art," embodies the element of time intertwined with space. It must be acknowledged that space-time motion not only is a matter of science: buy it also is of aesthetic and emotional matters. Motion, real or imaginary, and the processes for achieving it become the Gestalt in vitality of fine art arrangement. The reward is dynamic and kinetic composition that rates high in distinction. Understanding and enjoyment on the part of the viewer require active participation instead of just passive appreciation, as in the past.

For emphasis and to conclude thoughts on vision in motion, the fourth dimension, consider a quote from the *Realist Manifesto* (Naum Gabo and Antoine Pevsner): "We free ourselves from the one-thousand-year old error of art, originating in Egypt, that only static things be its elements. We proclaim that for present day perceptions, the most important elements of art are the kinetic rhythms." This statement is indeed profound if we apply it. As arrangers, let us rise to the challenge.

The Sensory Arts of Light and Sound

Our creative design concepts of today include many designs that are dependent on sensory reactions in their construction. Let us evaluate the sensory process, then apply it to our creative designs.

Definitions (*The American Heritage Dictionary*):

- Sensory: Any of the animal functions of hearing, sight, smell, touch and taste.

- Sensuous: Of, pertaining to, or derived from the senses. Having qualities that appeal to the senses. Readily susceptible through the senses.

- Light: Electromagnetic radiation that has a wave length in the range from about 3900 to about 7700 angstroms and that may be perceived by the unaided normal eye.

- Sound: A vibratory disturbance in the pressure and density of a fluid or in the elastic strain in a solid, with frequency in the approximate range between 20 and 20,000 Hertz capable of being detected by the organs of hearing.

Manufactured light that affects floral design is classified as:

- Incandescent: A concentrated direct source of warm yellow light.

- Fluorescent: Soft and diffused light that creates a bluish-gray cast on objects. There are other types of manufactured lights, such as black light, colored spots, strobe lights, etc.; however, these are used primarily for special effects.

Angle of projection is important to the designer because of the various effects this direction has on the overall design. Designs may be lighted from any angle, (above, behind, in front, etc.), depending upon the effect desired.

Lighting characteristics may affect designs in the following ways:

- Change the color of materials

- Dramatize an exhibit

- Create shadows

- Portray emotional impact and convey moods

- Enhance form and/or modify form

- Enrich textures

- Affect depth

Lighting effects are determined by several factors:

- Candle power and number of lights

- Type of light produced, by bulb(s) or tube(s), cellophane covered or filtered, warm or cool, ultraviolet or black, flashing or blinking, one color or a combination, etc.

- Distance from source and angle of projection

- Distribution (concentrated or diffused) and intensity (bright or dim)

The principles of design must be applied in selecting and using light. Care must be exercised, as some lighting equipment may be hazardous if handled improperly. Special lighting effects for flower shows should follow local fire codes and be compatible with electrical capacity of the facilities where the show is held.

Sunrise, sunset and auroral displays are nature's grandest manifestations of colored light. Fire, on all scales, perhaps led man to his first experiments in controlling light patterns. Adding chemicals to fire can change the flame color or can change the amount and color of the smoke. These effects, of course, would never be used in a flower show. With either a fire or a torch, shadows in motion can be produced by moving an object whose shadow is cast, or by moving sources of light. Only recently has electricity made simple and controllable light sources possible for artistic purposes.

Many who have studied vision, light and optics in the past have recognized the artistic potentialities of light in motion; however, an adequate review of kinetic art with light has yet to be written. Thomas Winfred was one of the first pioneers of this art form to produce generally satisfying results. Winfred advocated the word *lumia* without actually defining specific devices. The surface on which images are projected is important. In flower arranging, this surface is considered to be the background.

The design listed in our *Handbook* that involves *lumia* is **Illuminary Design**, a Creative Design incorporating light(s) as one of the components. The lighting must be an integral part of the design, not something added for the sole purpose of including light. Mechanics of including special lighting, such as wires and batteries, must be concealed or be an appropriate part of the design. Emphasis is placed on color, pattern and balance. Lights may be concealed within bases, and/or containers, or in the background, underlay or other components. These

designs are not to be confused with those having spotlights used from the front to enhance the overall design. Other design styles may have lighting incorporated, unless the schedule prohibits.

Sound, the second sensory art we are considering, is found listed in our *Handbook* under **Vibratile**, a Creative Design characterized by vibration and sound (see Chapter 6).

Creative Designs are often a combination of styles; therefore use of light, sound, and motion are not restricted to these named styles.

Figure 89.

A variety of interesting plant materials and other interesting objects are combined in a dynamic abstract Assemblage. The groupings of soft beige materials in the center of the design reflect light, as does the interestingly textured background.

Dynamic rhythm is carried throughout the overall design.

CHAPTER EIGHT

Decisions . . . Decisions

The Obligation of Being a Good Flower Show Judge

A quote from Mrs. Muriel Merrell, former National Council Judges Chairman: "Our *Hand-book* is our first guide for ideal judging techniques. Unfortunately we tend to speed read the material on good judging practices, in a rush to get to the magic of Design or Horticulture."

In these times of unrest and negative force, judges could accomplish a great deal through applied kindness. Comments to the exhibitors should be kind, sympathetic, and always express appreciation for one or more good points, perhaps about the container, the color concept or even clever mechanics. Be alert to the innovative and unusual. Our appreciation will do much to encourage the production of flower shows, and we do need them to further our knowledge and training. We should do as much as we can to make flower shows fun!

Fundamentally, a good judge of flower shows seeks out the maximum beauty of each exhibit and rewards it. Strive to be flexible and willing to adjust an earlier opinion. No one person has all knowledge, nor can one person see everything from one vantage point. One judge may see something not apparent to the other members of the panel, which is why we rely upon a consensus decision.

The basic quality underlying all good judges' public relations is the ability to work well with others. Understanding, thoughtful and considerate judges do not in any way offend their fellow team members. A judge's courage is rooted in knowledge. Speak from an informed background, and be prepared to back up your statements with facts and appropriate references, if needed. Never speak from personal likes or dislikes. Be prepared to give reasons for your decisions; these reasons should be stated to encourage rather than discourage.

Be tactful when you must disagree, and be willing to hear the other side. Discussion should not become mere bickering, with disparaging remarks bandied about. Point Scoring will clarify and point up merits or faults. Point scoring involves the use of a score card upon which certain qualities deemed important by the makers are allotted points to total 100, or ideal, perfection. In the act of judging, these scales draw attention to details that might be overlooked. With experience, it will not be necessary to actually add up the points unless the competition is very close. In such cases, the judges should break down the qualities and allot points to substantiate the fact that the decision is based on all the qualities as outlined in the scale. Ask questions if some point needs personal clarification, for no one can be expected to remember everything. It is no ill reflection to admit the limits of knowledge; the error lies in the failure to do something about it.

A Student Judge must be allowed and encouraged to express his/her opinion. Any one of a panel who is not allowed to state an opinion while point scoring is then not a working member, and the other judges are going contrary to the rules. On the other hand, beginning

judges often have a tendency to be too strict and technical and to exert too many rules. Experience usually will bring a more tolerant understanding.

Judging is a methodical, reasoned appreciation, with tolerance for minor infractions of a principle. If beauty and distinction have been achieved, give credit and appreciation for the skill involved. Look first to see and praise what has been done, rather than to criticize. What may seem at first to be design deficiencies may be a more creative approach. The too conservative judge is restrained by rules and maintains a level of mediocrity. The progressive judge aids advancement and development through expert evaluation and the realization that there are many ways the artistic exhibitor may treat a subject, within the latitude of the principles of design.

A judge's fitness for the task should have been determined upon acceptance of the judging invitation, at which time the ethical judge refuses any assignment for which he/she feels inadequate.

When decisions are based on appropriate standards, they represent wise judgment. Haphazard choices based on guesses, rationalization or whims are of little value. The actual act of judging is an operation of the mind, involving comparison to an ideal and evaluation of merit, out of which definite conclusions are reached. If each panel member is well-trained, experienced and conscientious, there will be no irreconcilable differences of opinion between them regarding the merits of the entries.

There is no such thing as a flexible decision. The first decision must be accurate and fair, for there is no chance of retraction after the ribbon has been placed. Factual discussion among the judges as to merits and demerits eases this decision-making task. By having all the facts in mind and talking over the entries with other members of the panel, each judge's thoughts are sorted out and clarified. While a judge should acquire reasonable speed in reaching a decision, it is discourteous to the conscientious judge for the team to hurry on to the next class before a decision is made known.

Judges often spend excessive time on the first few entries. Too much discussion over any one class is never desirable or fair to all exhibitors. If the judges know the number of classes and the amount of total time, they can determine whether five or fifteen minutes can be spent on each class.

If the judges find an exhibit that does not conform to the schedule, they may, out of courtesy, ask the committee to reclassify it to a more fitting one. However, a misplaced exhibit cannot be moved to a class already judged, which would make rejudging necessary.

Figure 90. (Opposite)

A beautiful example of repetition in a design, in which the rounded forms of the twisted vine repeat the rounded arch of the container. All principles of design are carefully observed.

Judges should not be expected to evaluate a design as it was before a line shifted, or a flower opened or withered, disrupting the balance. A judge evaluates only what is present at the moment of judging. Firmness and courage are necessary, because an honest judge will refuse to give in to improper requests. He/she will refuse to place unearned rewards.

When a class has been properly judged, there is seldom any question by competing exhibitors or a visitor as to the decision. However, should a question be raised, the careful and courteous judge should be able to promptly point out valid reasons for a decision, using words and manners that are intended to be helpful, rather than to cause resentment.

National Council of State Garden Clubs, Inc. has strict rules for the presentation of the coveted Top Exhibitor Awards. Judges should not hesitate to withhold these if no exhibit meets the stated requirements or if the exhibits are inferior.

All judges should agree on what is to be said if the clerks are to be instructed on what comments to write on the entry cards. Clear, well-written comments compliment the exhibitor. Sarcastic comments demean the judges. The time element necessitates concise, precise statements, pared down to the essentials. There is no time to write a lecture, and the judge should avoid giving a verbal one to clerks, delaying the judging. The written words should be definite, expressing the meaning as precisely as possible.

Suggestions for better commenting:

■ Instead of EXCELLENT:

admirable	extraordinary	notable	splendid
distinguished	flawless	outstanding	superb
elegant	illustrious	perfection	superlative
exceptional	incomparable	prominent	superior
exquisite	magnificent	remarkable	unequivocal
			utmost

"Reveals clear understanding of design"   *"Gratifyingly proportioned"*

"Delightful interweaving of related qualities"   *"Comprehensive understanding"*

"Unerring sense of appropriateness"   *"Remarkable degree"*

"Correctly simulates natural growth"   *"High order of excellence"*

"Recurrent qualities easily discernible"   *"Notably effective"*

"Undeniable relationships"   *"Dazzlingly dramatic"*

"Exceedingly good"   *"Compels admiration"*

"High degree of perfection"   *"Deliberately exciting"*

"Masterfully handled"   *"Consistent style"*

"Free from imperfections"   *"Skilled technique"*

■ Instead of GOOD:

acceptable	comfortable	enchanting	pleasant
accurate	commendable	evident	proper
adequate	competent	exact	qualifies
agreeable	complete	fair	satisfactory
ample	conform	favorable	skillful
apparent	correct	lovely	sound
appropriate	definite	obvious	sufficient
attractive	effective	passable	suitable
			unmistakable

"Relationship of likeness"   *"Agreed in purpose"*   *"Decided rhythmic flow"*

"Recurrent qualities"   *"Well-adjusted"*   *"Special consistent quality"*

"Sense of rightness"   *"Gratifying unity"*   *"Reasonable relationships"*

"Sense of fitness"   *"Well-adapted"*   *"Easily discernible"*

"Reflects good taste"   *"Well-qualified"*   *"Unified expression"*

"Meaningful relationships" *"Sufficient strength"*   *"Well suited to given purpose"*

■ Instead of POOR:

artlessness	disordered	incompatible	offending
awkward	displeasing	inconsistent	perplexing
clumsy	disturb	insignificant	second-rate
conflicting	ill-contrived	insufficient	superficial
confused	ill-suited	lacking	unfavorable
deficient	imperfect	meager	ungainly
disassociated	improper	meager	unnatural
disconnected	inadequate	meager	unrelated
disjointed	incomplete	misapplies	unsuitable
			weak

"Conflicting qualities"   *"Serves no constructive purpose"*

"Lacks inherent likeness"   *"Feeling of insecurity"*

"Includes irrelevant materials"   *"Loosely knit"*

"Lacking in certain quality"   *"Strength dissipated by over-elaboration"*

The judge is obligated to know the principles of design so well that his/her comments fit the subject. Statements must be logical, reasonable and tailor-made for each exhibit. They must be correct and lucid, and easily verified by observing the exhibit. To say, "It is a good design," is not really a statement of merit. Though it sounds complete, it conveys nothing, and upon analysis it leads to questions of why and how. No matter what the style of design, judges are concerned with:

- *Conformance to a schedule*

- *Interpretation of theme*

- *Competence of design, handling of color*

- *Condition of materials (damaged or wilted)*

- *Originality of concept and distinction in execution*

- *Artistic in concept*

Figure 91.

A design of beautifully coordinated components. Certainly "well suited to a given purpose," which is the creation of a bold and exciting design.

Within the general historical process, there are complex variations that arise fundamentally from the differences in individual psychology, from difficulties of communication and from physical variations of all kinds. To distinguish between general influences and personal indebtedness in any particular case is almost impossible. However, it is your duty as a judge to arm yourself with boundless quantities of knowledge in any and every subject related to your chosen field When the situation arises that we are confronted with making a decision or answering a question, we must combine knowledge with tact and consideration, then answer with action and motivation. When we do this, we will then be worthy of the honor bestowed upon us in being selected to guide the exhibitors of tomorrow.

Figure 92.

A design that is highly "artistic in concept" incorporates boldly rhythmic forms with exquisite contrasts in texture. The color harmony is appealing.

This beautiful design, created by Bob Thomas, was selected to be reproduced as a bronze sculpture.

A gift of Bob's many friends and admirers, the sculpture will be placed in the gardens at the Headquarters of National Council of State Garden Clubs, Inc. as a memorial to him.

In Remembrance of Bob Thomas

I have fought a good fight, I have finished my course, I have kept the faith.
II Timothy: 4,7.

Bob Thomas fought a short, but very intense and courageous fight against cancer. Unfortunately, this was a battle he could not win. To the great sorrow of his many friends, Bob finished his course in death on September 28, 1997.

The loss of Bob Thomas will leave a void in the hearts of all of us, and in the functioning of National Council of State Garden Clubs, Inc. He served NCSGC and its members devotedly and well for many years. Bob played such a broad and varied role in so many aspects of our organization that we will always be in his debt.

Bob Thomas was a huge man in many ways: in size; in a tremendous capacity for the enjoyment of life, expressed by his joyous, ringing laugh; in his great appreciation and expression of beauty; in his loyalty to friends; and in his capacity for cool reasoning and solid common sense. He possessed an enormous talent for creative design, which enriched the lives of so many people with whom he shared it. No doubt, each one who knew him will carry some special and unique memory from having known Bob.

Typically, at the time of his death, Bob was working on a number of projects that were important to him. His dream was to write a book on creative design, and he left many pictures and notes for such a book. As payment of our many debts to him, we will continue his works and will complete them to the best of our abilities.

Farewell, dear friend. You have kept the faith, and so shall we.

June Wood

June Wood
Vice President
National Council of State Garden Clubs, Inc.

INDEX